THE
PA'S
STORY

SEX, SALARIES AND
SQUARE MILE SLEAZE

THE PA'S STORY

SEX, SALARIES AND SQUARE MILE SLEAZE

V. A. KNOWLES

JOHN BLAKE

Published by John Blake Publishing Ltd,
3 Bramber Court, 2 Bramber Road,
London W14 9PB, England

www.johnblakebooks.com

www.facebook.com/johnblakebooks 🔲
twitter.com/jblakebooks 🔲

This edition published in 2015

ISBN: 978-1-78418-383-7

British Library Cataloguing-in-Publication Data:

A catalogue record for this book is available from the British Library.

Design by www.envydesign.co.uk

Printed in Great Britain by CPI Group (UK) Ltd

1 3 5 7 9 10 8 6 4 2

Papers used by John Blake Publishing are natural, recyclable products made from
wood grown in sustainable forests. The manufacturing processes conform to the
environmental regulations of the country of origin.

Every attempt has been made to contact the relevant copyright-holders, but some
were unobtainable. We would be grateful if the appropriate people could contact us.

CONTENTS

INTRODUCTION

I'll be honest. I'm really quite enjoying the anonymity of being a temp. I began working as a temp on Tuesday this week and before Tuesday I had not done a temporary job in over 10 years. I had just eaten my lunch in the breakout area of my current place of work. I had a freshly made bacon and avocado sandwich as bought from an overpriced City-based sandwich chain just up the road. I sat alone on a sofa in front of a huge plasma TV and must have looked like a sore thumb next to the other random employees who had all decided to sit around the canteen style tables to eat their lunch instead. I ate my sandwich whilst playing on my iPhone and I dropped bits of crispy bacon, avocado and crumbs down my black rain coat, whilst intermittently wiping my mayonnaise tarnished lips.

Ten years ago I might have given a shit about what I looked like or what others thought of me. Today I absolutely loved the fact that I didn't care what anyone thought of me. That is the beauty of being a temp. You are replaceable in peoples' minds. They don't feel the need to get to know you and vice versa. You are seen as not quite the full package and possibly a bit weird, which is why you have to temp in the first place.

At least, I'm sure that's what they think.

CHAPTER ONE

My boss is an arsehole. A proper bell-end. I cannot quite believe that it is happening again, but it is. This is my third job in just over two years. My CV is starting to look incredibly flaky. I left my last job because my boss was evil. I left the job before that because my boss was a bell-end *and* evil, and now I have just stepped into the lion's den yet again to find the devil himself masquerading as my boss. My innerself has just sighed heavily.

I am a PA (Personal Assistant) sometimes known as an EA (Executive Assistant), although to be honest I have never really known the difference between the two. I think some people like to be known as an EA, as it sounds more exciting, but in reality, whether you are one or the other, it's still the same job. You still get the same attitude and sometimes a moody boss and essentially you are still just someone's servant, no matter what you call yourself on your CV.

I didn't set out to be this person when I used to dream of what I'd do when I was older. I started life wanting to be Julie Andrews. I went to college and did theatre studies, then University to study performing arts and finally drama school to learn how to act. Unfortunately drama school didn't teach me how to act, it merely wiped out all of my natural instinct and replaced it with nerves and the inability to express any emotion on stage without simultaneously wondering where my 'centre' was, and whether the veins in my neck were sticking out because I wasn't using the secondary breathing technique – because these things *always* cross your mind in the heat of a real argument. I don't suppose it helped much either that ten minutes before the curtains went up on my graduation show, my tutor decided to shove his tongue down my throat. Why he decided to do this at that particular moment, I'll never know, but it didn't really do much more than confuse the hell out of me and ensure that the words 'drama school' would bring me out in cold sweats forevermore. Having graduated, I stepped out into the big bad world and whisked myself off to London to find the bright lights. I was excited to be there and couldn't wait for the next stage of my life to begin.

I slept on the living room floor of my friend Doug's flat in Stoke Newington for two weeks. I managed to get a job before a flat, which was a bit odd, but somehow it worked. I felt very grown up and was thrilled with my first proper job. I had previously only worked as a waitress and a shop assistant whilst at drama school and really had no idea what real office workers were like. I'm not sure to this day I can compare this first job to a real office either, because technically it was a call centre. Is that an office? Anyway, it was a call centre and I got the job on the strength of a telephone interview (luckily, given the nature of the job). My old friend from secondary school also worked there (having graduated from the same drama school as me the year before) and had told me they were always recruiting and were really flexible about you taking time off for auditions and as I was *clearly* going to be attending a lot of those, it was probably the best option, I surmised. I started at Telecall in the October of 1999 on five pounds an hour. I was rich beyond my wildest dreams.

Telecall felt like being at school. I sat in a chair for seven hours a day with a telephone headset clamped to my ear, waiting for the beep to indicate an inbound call had come in. I was trained on two separate campaigns; one for a very large electricity company, the other, a car manufacturer. I had a cushy job. I knew that the calls that came through to me were not going to be as unpleasant as the calls you had to make if you were on the outbound desk. If a call came through on inbound, you at least knew there was already a reasonable degree of interest in the product or service you were about to start blathering on about to them. The computerised voice would tell you which product the call was about before the caller started talking, so you could switch between the appropriate scripts on screen, before answering. In between taking calls, I used to pass the time with my friend by challenging him to see who could get down from the highest setting on the adjustable office chairs in the most amount of depressions on the hydraulic arm rests. That and seeing how many times I could put my other colleague off his call by saying the word 'bush' in a stupid voice. Why bush? I don't know. All I do know is that it worked and he had to terminate more than one phone call through laughing, which entertained me no end.

I giggled throughout my days at Telecall. The work was a piece of piss for regular people, but even easier for 'trained' actors, because the more we were able to add a flourish to our scripted sales talk, the more interesting our sales patter sounded and the more leads we converted, which in turn meant that the bosses liked us. On Fridays the downstairs kitchen and breakout area became a party. It was a weekly tradition that the management bought us beers and wine, and most people from the company started their weekends drinking together at 5pm before heading off to the pub to continue long into the night. In the early days of being in London this seemed so exciting and fun. By the time I was a regular at Telecall, I had moved into a flat with my then boyfriend, in Dulwich.

Poor Nick never really stood a chance with me. I'd met him at drama school and had really - really *liked* him — but never loved him and certainly never felt romantic about him, much as I tried to. He had declared his undying interest and fascination with me on the basis of a poem I had chosen to read in class one day. I was flattered so I had agreed to go out with him. We had agreed to move to London with a small group of friends from drama school upon graduating and just weeks before the big move, pretty much everyone had dropped out to pursue other things. The only other person left was my friend Emma who at the last minute decided she was going to go to India to get married.

So it left just Nick and me to move in together. Not the greatest of ideas when one half of the couple thinks its love and the other secretly wants it to be platonic. We had separate bedrooms. I knew he was in love with me. I stayed out practically every single Friday night getting hammered with my work mates. I never thought twice about Nick, or what I was doing to him. I was very selfish. I was still young, living in London, making money and then spanking every last penny on beer. Nick had not managed to secure any type of job and started to have the most dreadful outbreaks on his face, through stress. The inevitable happened one Friday. I kissed my boss, Mike, through a haze of Stella Artois. I'm not suggesting it was inevitable that I would kiss my boss; just that something was bound to happen on one of those drunken Friday evenings after work. Mike was a team leader, only three years my senior. Nick moved out, Mike moved in and then my life started to fall apart.

CHAPTER TWO

I realise now that my time at Telecall was really just one big party. I never took it seriously. I worked to buy booze, drink and socialise, but it was always with my work colleagues. I never looked at the bigger picture. I never met anyone new and I lost touch with all of my friends from University, who had been living in London for a few years.

I was living with Mike, who turned out to have an aircraft hangar of emotional baggage, a seriously grim addiction to Benson and Hedges fags and someone who thought it quite normal to march me from one end of the corridor in our flat to the other, without my feet even touching the floor, until the force of him slamming my back against the locked cellar door would burst open, allowing us both to tumble arse over tit down concrete steps until we dropped to the damp, hard floor. I was bruised by him regulary, but was so weak emotionally that I didn't have the strength to leave or ask him to leave. Instead, what little money we both earned, we spent on booze.

We drank to escape the pain of the fights and all that was wrong in our relationship, but all it did was make us like each other for a while until the nasty stage of being drunk would rock up to say hello. Then it would start all over again. I ended up having more and more days off work and, eventually, I was told that I wasn't needed any more. Our relationship ended. I had no job and I was seriously depressed. I moved back home to live with my mum, carrying just a suitcase of my belongings. The rest of my things were left rotting in the damp cellar at the flat that was my first London address. I never did recover them; which means that somewhere out there is an audio cassette tape of me and my school friends absolutely battered and a limited edition of Madonna's 'Sex' book, covered in mildew and cobwebs.

Being back at my mums was the break that I had needed. I knew it was only going to be short-term as I was determined to move back to London eventually. After three months of home cooking, temporary work and some much needed TLC, I made the move back to London via a stint at Brunel University. I wasn't a student though. I had applied to work for a company who provide English study holidays for overseas children each summer at various institutes across the UK. I was the Social Organiser in charge of all the trips that were arranged for the students throughout their two week stay with us. Trips to places like Leeds Castle and Thorpe Park.

If anyone hasn't heard of these types of companies who provide these programmes, I highly recommend them. They are a great introduction to work, you get paid well, your food and board is provided and you get to meet some really interesting, lovely people. I worked and lived at Brunel for two months altogether. Every Friday I got paid £75 in cash from my weekly wage so I could spend on site at the student bar or shop. I attended discos, used the gym, had parties and nights out locally with all the other staff members and truly had a great time. It was just what I had needed after my horrendous time with Mike, but as with all good things, it had to come to an end and so two months after starting, I found myself making the move back to London, full of trepidation.

As with my first job in London, my second came via my old school friend again, who by now had also moved on from Telecall. He was now working in another call centre in Islington. Through him, I was offered a job there too and I managed to rent a single room in an ex-council flat in Kennington, sharing with the guy who owned it. It wasn't glamorous and my new flat mate was a complete pain-in-the-arse, anally retentive dick that had to poke his nose into my business every minute of every day. I had only my suitcase of belongings, a single bed and no curtains in my room. In the new job I would work on a Saturday and so had one day off in the week to compensate. I chose Wednesdays as my regular day off, which meant Tuesday nights were my night to enjoy myself. With the small amount of money I made, I had very little to spend on myself after paying my rent and share of the bills, so all I could afford to do on a Tuesday was buy a bottle of white wine and ten cigarettes. I would then sit in my single room watching terrestrial TV, slowly drinking and smoking out of my bedroom window until I was happily drunk. When I had been working for a few weeks I bought myself a new video recorder from Argos, so at least I could vary what I watched whilst getting pissed. I was genuinely quite happy, even though this now sounds like the saddest existence ever.

The call centre was an inbound complaints line for a huge British institution. It handled some other calls, but complaints were the main bread and butter. 4,000 came in every day. I discovered whilst in this job, that I was quite good at what I did. When I started, I was immediately put on the mainline. Mainline is the lowest rung of the ladder. You had a headset glued to your ear and had to answer every call that came through and deal with it. If you had a particularly taxing call you could press the 'not ready' button which meant that no calls would come into you. The only time apart from that, when you could place yourself on 'not ready' was when you went to the loo. They employed people to monitor the lines and if you were ever on 'not ready' for longer than five minutes, they came looking for you to ask why.

It was hard work. This was the entire UK at its grumpy best, calling to have a massive pop at you. You were representing a national service that was failing badly. The hatred flowed, the sarcasm and anger steamed and on more than one occasion, I had to deal with someone sobbing down the line.

I hadn't been on mainline for very long when I was asked to

have a chat with Pam Peacock. She was known throughout the call centre for being a complete bitch. I was trying to think of a kinder way to describe her then, but to be honest my memory of her just doesn't deserve the recognition. Think 'Vinegar Tits' from Prisoner Cell Block H, in a shell suit. That was Peacock. I was a little nervous at the prospect of meeting her at first, but realised that I hadn't done anything wrong so I couldn't possibly be in trouble. Peacock and I met. It turned out that I had indeed been recognised as being good on the phones and I was therefore being asked to join the more prestigious 'Products' line which meant only a handful of calls a day and from nice people who actually wanted your advice on something, rather than wanting to bite your head off.

It did strike me as a little silly that when I was as good as I was at dealing with upset and irate customers; they thought it best to whisk me off and put me in a gilded cage to do a job that required very little. Surely this would just mean that the staff that stayed on the mainline taking complaints weren't really that good with customers, and in turn that would just reinforce the pre-conception that the company was indeed rubbish? Regardless, it was no longer my issue and I joined the products line the following week, under the leadership of Pam Peacock.

Things started off well on the products line. I liked the guys I sat with, there was plenty of office banter to see you through the boring bits and I ended up learning new skills that I could add to my CV. My social life picked up again through regular

Friday nights in the pub with my new work buddies. I began to think that I might like this work malarkey after all, but it slowly became apparent that my old schoolmate who I had started working with again, might be the kryptonite to my Superman. I suppose I was getting a little bit older and wiser.

While my friend was becoming more and more frustrated with life, I was beginning to think that I could do a lot more with mine. We still went out drinking together at the weekends, usually at a gay bar, but more and more often he would not turn up to work at all and it just wasn't me to be that person anymore. I didn't want to live like a student still, getting hammered, not turning up for work and then drinking more to escape the next day's guilt. It was a sad existence when I truly looked at it. My friend made noises about just leaving London for Australia to escape it all. He asked if I wanted to go, but the bottom line was that you needed to show savings in excess of two thousand pounds before you could travel on a working visa and I just didn't have that kind of money, nor could I borrow from anyone. On the other hand, he had a well-off father who could lend him the money.

About three months after first talking about it, he left for Sydney via Kuala Lumpur. I watched the huge Malaysian Airlines plane depart whilst standing on the viewing platform at Heathrow and felt a lump in my throat. I knew I was pretty much alone in London again. For all of the craziness that he still craved and I did not, he had still been my rock throughout such bad times with my ex, Mike. He had been there for me through the tears and meltdowns and I had probably spent every single weekend with him after Mike and I had split, getting wrecked in one way or another and having the biggest laugh, but I knew I needed to stay and make something of myself. Running away to another country wasn't an option for me.

I carried on working at the call centre and life just trotted on by for a while. Pam Peacock wore the same shell suit every day. On Saturdays she seemed a little bit more chilled and would often regale us with stories of her non-existent love life. I recall a rather special Saturday when Pam informed us that her vagina had grown moss over its entrance as it had been so long since it had been penetrated. She was a proper filthy bitch and rumour had it that she was actually knobbing one of the delivery men who brought the stationery supplies late on a Friday. How true that was, I'm not sure, but according to my team leader, she had been caught on all fours once with her shell suit bottoms around one ankle, howling like a dog whilst Terry Dinnage had pounded her from behind on top of a roll of bubble wrap. With each movement you could hear it being popped, apparently. I'm presuming it worked well as a surface too, because aside from the comfort factor, it was wipe-clean. Handy.

The call centre used a separate company based in Manchester to mystery shop us sporadically. They brought a new policy in that now meant on answering a call you had to say 'Good morning/afternoon, Customer Services Products line, my name is John Smith, how can I help you?' Now I'm sorry, but that is just too much of a mouthful if you ask me.

I personally hate it when I call a customer service number and someone takes that long to introduce themselves before I can even speak. It just seems too awkward and I feel a bit embarrassed for the person on the other end having to say it.

But, regardless, I did start saying the full intro and continued doing so, until one particular afternoon when someone called and I answered, but stumbled at the first hurdle and messed up all of my words which made both me and my caller laugh. I apologised and simply said something like 'you've reached blah blah customer services, how can I help?' It would have felt so stupid, false and forced had I started it all again from the beginning as I am sure most normal, rational people would agree. Little did I know, however, that my afternoon caller was in fact a mystery shopper from Manchester. And what did my lovely mystery shopper do? She bloody well reported me for not having used my full name on answering my call!

So, the next day Pam Peacock was on the bloody rampage, wasn't she? I don't know why I didn't admit it at first, but as Pam kept asking who *hadn't* given their full name, I didn't say anything. I probably just thought it was such a petty incident that she'd drop it in the end. She did not drop it though and her anger was such that her incessant pacing caused enough friction for her shell suit to be in danger of catching fire; so I had to confess. I honestly thought that she would understand why I had abandoned my full intro. She didn't. She found none of it funny. She was furious. It was the first time in my working life that I really resented being somewhere and working for them. She spoke to me like a child and I muttered a few things under my breath and she then threatened to send me back to the 'mainline'. So I muttered some more stuff under my breath and I swear I could see sparks starting to come off the shell suit. She told me to get my things and go back onto the mainline, like it was a bloody punishment!

The next bit I remember very clearly, because instead of muttering, I said loud and clear "Fuck this" and turned my PC off. That is when old Peacock turned nasty. She simply couldn't abide that fact that I was terminating my employment and not her. Her face turned a violent shade of red and she told me I was fired; to which I replied that she couldn't fire me as I had clearly just quit. I then found myself matching her anger with pure calm. The more wound up she became, the easier I found it to stay absolutely in control, which she hated. I took my time gathering my belongings and all the while she made a song and dance about me being fired and that I needed to leave now and the longer I stayed, the more irate she became and threatened to call security – security for what?!

It was so ridiculous it was actually funny, although inside I was secretly shaking because I really did think she was going to hit me. Her final attempt at insulting me, was when she told me that everybody on my team 'hated me', so I made sure I took extra time to go and say goodbye to my work buddies one by one and hug the people who I had become close to. I waltzed slowly out of the call centre under her steely gaze and felt daggers piercing my back, but knew I was the victor.

Looking back, I guess Pam Peacock was the first knob-head

boss, but I hadn't had my fingers burned badly enough at that stage to be seriously concerned about what the next job might bring. Plus, as the work had been long-term temping, I had always had the safety net in the back of my mind that I could just walk out if it wasn't working for me. The only thing that I didn't like about temping was the fact that the pay was so rubbish. I figured at about this time that it was obvious I wasn't going to get my big acting break anytime soon and after a long think, I decided that I actually wanted a bit more stability in my life. I signed up to a few recruitment agencies and asked to be considered for permanent jobs which I knew would bring a better wage. I didn't care what the job was; I just applied for anything and everything within administration.

After a couple of weeks I was asked to interview for a role as a receptionist and property assistant at the Primrose Hill branch of a well-known estate agents. I got the job and felt very grown up and absolutely petrified at the same time. I had hardly any proper work clothes. One pair of trousers that I owned was the type that looked shiny and melted onto your iron if you went higher than a silk setting. The other pair was less shiny, but the hem on the bottom kept falling down and I repeatedly had to stick it back up with double sided sticky tape. My mum had to take me shopping for a suit. She could barely afford to buy herself clothes, but she was so sweet and so pleased that I had a job with a reputable firm, that she threw caution to the wind and put the suit onto her Debenhams store card.

CHAPTER THREE

I started my first permanent job on a salary of £18,000. It was quite a novelty to be paid monthly for a change. The commute to work wasn't that bad. I was travelling from Kennington to Primrose Hill on the northern line and it didn't take that long. The work wasn't bad either. Aside from the usual typing and answering of phones, I was in charge of meeting and greeting the passers-by who walked in without appointments, as well as those who had booked.

Being one of the high-end estate agents in Primrose Hill, a lot of celebrities used to come by. A singer from a famous band really liked one of the agents on house sales and used to greet him with a massive bear hug. A famous British actor wandered in one Saturday asking for details on a particularly lavish and expensive house on the Bishops Avenue, and the wife of a famous chef used to rock up with her kids too.

I do remember feeling slightly embarrassed one afternoon when an actress from Coronation Street walked in though. I shook her hand when she came in. I clearly remember thinking what terribly dry hands she had, which removed some of the showbiz shine for me. She asked about flats for sale in the region of about £250,000. I had to tell her that we didn't have any flats below a starting price of £400,000 and her face fell. She left without details of anything. It seems ridiculous now that even back then you couldn't buy anything for less than that.

What of my boss though? Was he an arsehole too? In short, the answer is no, I wouldn't class him as an arsehole. More of a pompous prick. As with most places of work that I ended up at, it is true to say that there was always 'one'. You can have a fellow work force consisting of ninety per cent decent people, but there will always be one person who really is a complete tosser. We've all had them. It doesn't have to be the boss, it could be a colleague, but I guarantee that if you think back about all the places you have worked before, I expect you can recall one person you wished you didn't have to work with. Let's face it, most of us aren't going to truly enjoy going to work on a daily basis to earn a piddling little salary, in return for doing repetitive mind-numbing tasks, but mostly it would just about be acceptable if you didn't have to then deal with an irritating little fucker who in reality you would never choose to talk to, let alone socialise with after work. There are a variety of tossers in the work place; no one shoe fits all and the word tosser doesn't actually do them all justice, but for now let me tell you about my boss at the estate agents.

Joe Kessler was a slim, well-dressed gay man in his late forties. He wore those thin rimmed round glasses and on first introduction could be quite intimidating. He looked at me as if I was an alien. He really didn't get me. He wasn't prepared to either. There was never any danger that I would get into a regular conversation about what I had done in my spare time or vice versa. He was definitely a 'children should be seen and not heard' believer, even if I happened to be a 25 year old woman.

I suppose I didn't really care at first, but then it really started to irritate me that every morning he would arrive and I would say 'good morning' to him and he would completely ignore me. I was such a smiley, friendly person. Every other person used to say hello to me. Not him. And no, it wasn't just the way he was, because he used to say hello to other people - just not me. I found him very rude and I wasn't used to being treated like that. I just didn't see how someone could be so dismissive. What really hacked me off was seeing the way he fawned over clients who came to the office. When he was approached by a hugely famous designer to personally find him a home in Primrose Hill, he could not have been more sycophantic. It was enough to make me want to vomit. I'm sure he probably harboured a secret fantasy that this client would fall madly in love with him, dress him in Gucci and whisk him away from the plebs in the office. In the end he didn't though, and in fact dropped Joe and used a different agent altogether for his house purchase.

Joe had his own secretary, Marcia. She had been with him

for years. She was a really nice woman; caring, understanding and she was Joe's right hand lady. Joe never asked me for a thing. He always took his work straight to Marcia, which suited me. One week when Marcia was on holiday, he reluctantly had to ask me to do some typing for him. I already did audio-typing for one of the other agents. Audio typing was easy. I was given a pre-dictated tape and would sit with my headphones on and type away in my own time, winding back and forth or slowing the speed right down with my foot pedal, trying to figure out what the voice had said at various garbled points.

There was no stress involved, because I typed in my own time at a pace that suited me. When Joe asked me to type he didn't give me a tape. Joe liked to dictate there and then. He didn't stand in front of me though. He stood right behind me and dictated as I typed. He also looked at every single thing I typed as it happened. It drove me mad.

Why the fuck couldn't he have been one of those business types you see in movies where they pace the office floor, whilst waxing lyrical and pausing dramatically every few moments to gather their thoughts and take in the view of a downtown metropolis? At least I would have had time to catch up and correct any typos as I went along. The very nature of someone dictating behind you puts you under so much pressure that you end up typing with all the accuracy of a chimp being zapped with a cattle prod. And that is what I did.

I kept making mistakes and at first he didn't say anything, but I sensed he wasn't happy, which just made it worse. I continued and gradually a few of his sighs crept in after each word I messed up. This only made it worse, because my hands then became slightly shaky and that meant more cock-ups on the keyboard. I could feel myself burning up under his watchful gaze and his sighs then turned into tuts, which after a few more mistakes turned into a combination of tuts and an exasperated "No!". Just as I thought he couldn't be more unimpressed with me, he let out a huge "No, dear!" in what was the most over-dramatised, sarcastic voice he could muster and I suddenly lost my rag spectacularly.

I stood up from my desk and told him I couldn't do it anymore. The tears which had been welling up suddenly burst through the flood barrier and as I gulped them back, I tried to put my thoughts into a normal voice, but failed miserably. Instead I took centre stage in the middle of the reception and said rather loudly 'You treat me like a piece of shit. Like I'm stupid, and I'm not'. I was possessed by the devil. Something beyond my control had told me to get up and stop taking this shit from him.

I recall Joe looking utterly horrified, but probably more so because the reception area was entirely glass-fronted and passers-by could clearly see in. God forbid Mr Charm should be seen to be the office bully. What would the celebrities think? He hurriedly spoke and said 'I'm dreadfully sorry, I absolutely did not mean to upset you, but could you please continue typing as this report needs to go out today'. So I did. I didn't know what else to do and I certainly had not planned on getting up from my desk and reacting so histrionically. I sat back down and god knows how I did it, but I continued typing and as I did, tears pattered softly onto my keyboard.

That really should have been that, but just as Joe and I thought it was all over, the devil inside me decided to speak again. I had for the last few minutes been silently playing out what had just happened in my head and suddenly felt the inexplicable urge to explain my theory. So again, speaking without thinking, I let Joe know that I was sorry and that it was probably because I was on my period. Just what he wanted to hear, I'm quite sure. I learned later on that the entire office downstairs had heard everything including the part about menstruation, which had caused the flat lettings girls to silently cry with laughter. Joe must have been mortified and secretly wondering why on earth he had ever employed me.

Joe was, however, altogether more approachable after that episode. He made the effort to say hello to me in the mornings and he never asked me to type another thing again for him. I even got a pay rise and a bonus. However, it was not enough to keep me. I had become bored of the same old routine as nothing was a challenge and I knew I was capable of a lot more. The company I worked for had an intranet. I used to look at it from time to time when things were slow in the office. Internal jobs were advertised on the site and one in particular caught my eye. It was for an advertising assistant in the marketing department. I applied for it and was invited for an interview. I got down to the last two, but didn't get the job. At least I could only presume that the job had gone to someone else, when I never heard back from the guy who had interviewed me.

Weeks went by and nothing, so I presumed the worst and carried on as normal. It was only at that year's Christmas party that I bumped into the man who had interviewed me and reminded him that he had never let me know. He was incredibly apologetic and very sheepish indeed. I thought no more of it until the New Year when his colleague telephoned me and asked if I had seen another role within marketing that had recently been advertised. I *had* actually seen it and had been interested, but had not applied for fear of being messed about again. Surprisingly, the guy who had initially interviewed me had actually put a good word in for me. I was asked if I would be applying for the job and I said that I would. After just one interview I was offered it. I could not have been more excited. I was the new National Advertising Coordinator on an improved salary of £20,000.

*

I started in my new role and had a handover of two weeks with the girl who had been doing the job for the last year. She was only leaving as she was off to study. I was fascinated by her. She was one of those types that defied all logic. She was super skinny, but had the biggest boobs I had ever seen and wasn't shy about putting them out there. I am talking super-sized. The job itself seemed enormous also, but one that I was confident I could do. It was interesting and pacey and I had real responsibility.

I was my own boss and was pretty much left to my own devices. If it all went wrong then it was my fault and I understood this and was more determined than ever to get a handle on things. I was in charge of all advertising for residential re-sale property across the UK. If someone from our Salisbury office for example, wanted to sell a property with a farm attached I got an advert in the *Farmers Weekly*; if the Knightsbridge office had a grand flat to sell, I got an advert in *Condé Nast*. Nothing happened if it didn't come through me first. I kept thinking that it must all be a mistake. Why on earth had they employed me with absolutely zero experience in this field?

It was at this stage of my life that I finally escaped from the oppressive guy I had been sharing with. He had sold his flat and was about to move to another equally rough area of London and fully expected me to move with him and continue to be his cash cow and general cleaner. It would have been easy to move with him and not go through the boring process of finding my own place to live, but I knew I had to escape. I had once again been surfing the company intranet and had seen an advert about a room within a family house in Battersea. It didn't sound ideal as I would be living with kids too, but the idea of living in a nicer area of London appealed, plus the advert did say own bathroom and large double room so I thought I would at least check it out.

I was not disappointed. The very lovely family (mum, dad and two children) lived in a grand, four storey town house on a lovely road near to the bustling bars of the Northcote

Road between Wandsworth and Clapham. It was perfect. I moved in and immediately felt more upwardly mobile. I was going places. I could afford a few more things now and I made new friends. I settled into my job more each day and felt good about myself. Even living with the family had its advantages. If I ever ran out of booze, they always offered me a bottle from their huge cellar and I bet what they gave to me was a lot better than I could normally afford. They were hugely generous.

Everything was great in my job until the day that Helen Martin appeared in the office, three months in. Helen had been employed as the new marketing manager for the company and had been brought in to replace the chap who had initially recommended me for my job. Helen was tall, slim and had short blonde hair, but had an unfortunate face with a very odd, over-sized jaw. She was a year younger than me. She was also now, effectively my boss. I was absolutely cool with this to begin with, I was happy to have another new person to talk to. Unfortunately Helen turned out to be the most irritating, insincere, horrible and ugly person, (both inside and out), that I had ever encountered.

Helen played it safe to begin with. Not showing her true colours at first. She sat next to me and was quite harmless. It didn't even register with me that she was my boss and that she actually was in charge of me and my work output. As far as I was concerned I was doing a good job and did not need any supervision. Helen wasn't in charge of just me, she was also expected to comment on and improve the whole team's work and at first I appeared to have escaped the Helen 'makeover'.

Helen was actually a highly intelligent person and to all intents and purposes was good at marketing. The problem with her was that she literally had no people management skills. There was no polite button. She was similar to a large, loud, angry animal who charged in at full throttle, barking her wisdom at you and if you didn't quite understand what she meant, or couldn't actually keep up with the speed at which she used to bark it out, she got really frustrated and treated you like you were stupid. This happened regularly to begin with and it really did not go down well with not only the marketing team, but also the PR team who were half way down the corridor and not under Helen's management at all. Nevertheless, Helen was the type to tell people exactly what she thought, whether having been asked for her opinion or not and PR soon got a taste of her medicine. The feathers were ruffled in marketing - to the point where a hate campaign started behind Helen's back.

There was a girl who sat opposite me who was so sickly sweet you just knew she had to be full of shit – and as I discovered, she was. Lucinda Timms was the type who just loved to be liked. She was a very posh girl from a very privileged background, who tried desperately to play this down and be one of 'us' and it fooled most people into thinking what a nice girl she was. In reality she was just a very bitter person, who despite everything life had given her, was a very plain Jane, who still had a chip on her shoulder from her days at school, where she had been bullied for being so short. Lucinda showed her true vindictive side when she started regularly emailing me and other people in the team whenever Helen spoke, inviting us all to ignore her or agree with her that she was a 'fucking prick'.

I was never going to be Helen's fan, but at this stage Helen had done nothing to warrant me actively disliking her, yet here was a girl who I barely knew, trying to coerce me into joining her bullying campaign against Helen. It simply felt wrong and it was the first time I questioned Lucinda's integrity and real motives. I would later go on to realise what a sneaky, two-faced bitch Lucinda really was.

What happened next was incredibly intriguing though. PR had decided that Helen was a thoroughly unpleasant person who had stepped on their shoes one too many times, so decided to take their complaints to our Managing Director, who turned out to be an even bigger dick than Helen. They had heard from various other offices that the dislike of Helen and her blunt managerial manner had gone UK-wide. The problem was that where the general people disliked her, the management loved her, because she was talking in their language. The majority of management was male and Helen spoke like a man and understood business like a man and more importantly, knew what strategy to take to make everyone more money. Management were not going to let a small thing like pissing the entire company off, get in the way of that. So, much to the dismay of Lucinda and the whole PR team, she stayed and continued to act in her brash manner.

Gradually it became apparent that although deeply unpopular, Helen was pretty untouchable and slowly one by one, people started to accept her for who she was and if I wasn't mistaken, they were actually starting to suck up to her. Just as I thought things were going to get back to normal, Helen decided that the way I worked needed to be addressed next. I had dodged Helen's interfering ways for a long time, until one day I called in sick with a migraine.

When I returned to the office, I opened up my emails to find that nothing was as I had left it. Helen quite happily told me what a mess my filing was and that she had called IT to get my password changed, so she could access my emails and had then completely re-vamped my whole set up. She had created sub-folders and had colour coded items. I did not recognise a thing, nor did I feel like my work was my own anymore.

It might sound dramatic, but I felt violated. This woman had gained access to my emails and had attacked the entire way in which I accessed and used them. She had taken my way of working and changed every single thing about it so that it made more sense to her, not me. It really might not seem much, but my job meant I had to be organised. I received a lot of email requests for advertising and if I didn't know what I was doing, then things fell apart pretty quickly and the company lost money. I had my own way of filing important documents and a system that enabled me to work efficiently. It was my job after all, so you would think that this might have been important. It's the equivalent of say, a baby sitter moving every bit of furniture around in your house and moving all items in your kitchen cupboards one night when you are out. You then come home to find nothing where it was or how you liked it and your baby sitter telling you they did it because it worked better for them that way and what's more, you should be grateful to them, because you will be a more efficient person now!

I was fuming.

And that was when it changed. That was when we locked horns and I decided I absolutely bloody hated her.

CHAPTER FOUR

Whether I showed too much of myself in the weeks and months to come I don't know, but Helen could see the effect that her meddling had on me and I presume it spurred her on to be even more interfering. I suppose I wasn't very good at hiding how I really felt. I had always been an open book and worn my heart on my sleeve. It made me vulnerable. She was so inconsistent because on the one hand she would be all over me and wanting to go for drinks with me and pretending to be my best friend and then she would behave in such a mean way towards me that it was impossible not to feel anything but vitriol for her.

Two examples of this come to mind. The first occasion was probably a good year into us working together. I had come to the conclusion that doing my job was never going to satisfy me like a creative outlet would, but rather than just accept it and be miserable, I was always trying to do something more. I was an optimist. I had recently bought a second hand Toshiba laptop via our company intranet. I paid only £50 for it. It was an absolute brick. Just typing the smallest amount of text took an age. The internal fans on it would fire up as if it was about to take off and there would be a good five second delay between me typing a sentence and the words eventually catching up and appearing on the screen.

Formatting was a different kettle of fish altogether. I could easily try and highlight something or change a load of text to italic or something similar, go to make a cup of tea and it still wouldn't be done by the time I came back. However, I was so pleased just to have a computer that nothing would dampen my spirit. I had been inspired by Matt Damon and Ben Affleck who wrote Good Will Hunting as a way of getting their voices heard. At this stage of my life I didn't think anyone was going to take me seriously as an actor as I had taken so much time off from even trying. I thought I was funny. I could act, so perhaps I should try and write something funny as a vehicle for me? And that is what I did, on my achingly slow lap top, night after night.

Quite how it came to light, I can't fully remember, but one Monday at work, I found myself talking about what I had done at the weekend and I mentioned my writing. Suddenly all ears pricked up and as usual, Helen had to get in on the conversation. I say conversation, but there really wasn't one. She simply heard what I was doing, laughed loudly and said

'Don't be ridiculous. You'll never finish that. I don't know why you are even trying'. Our office was open plan and so there was no escaping people or their opinions if you didn't like them.

Everyone could hear Helen. It wasn't the first time she tried to put me down in front of others. My love life or lack of was always fair game for her. I couldn't win. If I didn't say who I fancied or was dating, I was 'uptight' and if I did mention anyone who I did like or had been on a date with, I got told to calm down and not get too excited because it would 'only end in tears'. I worked with Helen for four years and as you might expect, I did date a few people in that time frame. I was nearing thirty, was single and living in London. I had resorted to internet dating because I just couldn't meet anyone unless I went to night clubs and quite frankly I couldn't be arsed with them, because unless you were wearing next to nothing, blokes used to just stare straight through me.

It was a very tough time for me. I was lonely. I used to cry myself to sleep some nights and ask someone out there to just magically produce someone to love me. I missed having a hug. So to have to deal with the sarcasm and sniping from Helen as well, was simply too much.

Another time that Helen was totally out of order was about three years in. I was unwell one day whilst out with a friend at lunch time. It was totally unexpected, as I had been feeling fine up until this point. We had gone to a bar for a quick drink as it was a Friday. For no apparent reason I became incredibly dizzy and felt very anxious. I suddenly felt as though someone had grabbed my entire surroundings and had spun them like a merry-go-round. It was terrifying. It only lasted a split second, but it was enough to drain the entire colour from my face. I became very giddy immediately afterwards and my friend noted how manic I seemed. Then it happened again and I honestly thought she was going to have to call an ambulance for me. It stopped as soon as it had started, but I felt dreadful and was petrified that it was going to keep happening.

My friend walked me back to work. As soon as some other members of staff saw me they put me on the floor and raised my legs and fed me with all manner of sweet things, thinking I had merely had a near fainting moment and needed sugar. It actually turned out to be a lot more than that. I was diagnosed with labyrinthitis when I eventually made it to my doctor. Labyrinthitis is an inner ear infection caused usually by a virus. There are no drugs you can take for it and no way of getting to the affected part as it is so far inside your head. The virus had caused damage to my right balance receptor, which is what had caused my two bouts of sudden vertigo. Your balance goes completely and it is one of the most horrible, scariest things to experience. Without balance you literally cannot function normally.

I had to take time off work because the only thing I could do was to sit it out and wait for the brain to catch up with what had happened and work out a way to re-balance me. I was in bed for two weeks. If you aren't careful, depression and anxiety can really take over. Nothing seemed real and from being an active person I was suddenly a bed-ridden recluse. I developed depression and suffered from anxiety. My doctor suggested I go on anti-depressants which I did; grateful for anything that would help me get back to normal.

Prozac was my saviour. I went back to work after just over two weeks. It was a bit hairy at first. I had to walk away from my computer and sit somewhere quiet every now and then, to compose myself. I was still not quite right and panicky. I made the mistake of telling Helen that I had been put on anti-depressants. This was a huge mistake. I should have known that as with everything else in life, she had a strong opinion on this too. She was totally against anyone taking them and she let me know in no uncertain terms, loudly and in front of the rest of the team. She even asked other people's opinions.

It was such a private and sensitive matter to me and I could not understand why anyone would feel it appropriate to do this. To hold debate over my life at a time when I was feeling so vulnerable was disgusting. I was so weak and she was such a forceful and scary cow that she made me agree in front of everyone that I would only take the anti-depressants for a month and then stop. It had been recommended by my doctor that I take it for at least three months to ensure that they worked. I was also told to come off them very slowly, reducing the dose as opposed to suddenly stopping; otherwise I might get side effects that might be worse than the depression itself. Yet here I was agreeing with everything Helen said.

I obviously wasn't going to follow Helen's 'advice', but it

was easier to agree with her than continue to have my private life pulled apart in front of everyone and quite frankly, I had no energy to argue back at that time anyway. When it came to getting my repeat prescription a month later, I had arranged to collect it from my local chemist at 8.15am enabling me to get to work for the normal time and not have to explain my late arrival into work.

Typically on the day I chose to collect the prescription, the pharmacist had not even arrived, so I had to wait. By the time she turned up it had gone past 8.30am. I was going to be late to work no matter what. I would have to tell Helen, but I couldn't think of any excuse and furthermore all I could think was why the hell should I have to lie anyway? It was just so ridiculous that I was being made to feel like a naughty school child when I was a grown woman and this was a private matter. I called her to tell her I was going to be late.

'Why, what's the matter' she asked.

'Nothing, I've had to come to collect a repeat prescription from my doctor, but the pharmacist was late so I am now late, sorry' I replied.

'What is the repeat prescription for' she enquired.

'It's for Prozac' I sighed.

'I thought we agreed you weren't going to take that any longer than a month' Helen barked at me.

Unbelievable. By the time I got to work, the bitch had told the entire department and I felt like a leper.

What was I supposed to do? What would anyone have done? This was my job and this was my boss. I was in a situation where I didn't know how to act or react. I was a normal, well-mannered person. I wouldn't have dreamt of interfering with someone else's life or commenting on it to such an extent, because I knew it was totally inappropriate, but here I was having to answer to Helen about every aspect of my life on a daily basis. She was a complete bitch. Nothing was sacred.

My love life, my health, my hobbies, my home, my banking arrangements. Everything. If it has never happened to you I suppose it is easy to say that you would have nipped it in the bud early and made sure she knew you wouldn't tolerate it; but she snuck up on me slowly. I found it so very difficult to say anything because I was always taken aback by her audacity. If I had been outside of work there is just no way I would have taken this amount of shit from someone. I would have let rip by now and torn a couple of strips off her, but this was work and she was in charge so I had to bite my tongue.

We all found out at some stage that Helen had medical issues; in fact, she was on medication herself. It dawned on me that she was bitter and possibly slightly envious of me. When Helen started I was full of beans and confident. I had a shitty love life yes, but I had a lot of friends, was reasonably attractive and talented. I was everything that Helen wasn't and she seemed determined to put me down.

She was in a relationship when she started working with me. We were half-way through our third year of working together when her boyfriend had to go for an operation, but we of course were not allowed to know what procedure he was having done. God forbid if I had asked her to discuss the private ins and outs in front of the whole team. It was only when he suddenly dumped Helen two months later, that it all came out about what he had done.

Ironically it was me who she had called on the morning that it had happened. She was in tears. Why me? It was all so strange, but as false as it seemed, I had to encourage her to come into work even though she felt bad. It turned out that her boyfriend of four years had been living with man breasts and had finally had the operation to get them removed. The extra confidence of finally having them removed had clearly given him the courage to get out of the relationship with Helen. Maybe he had only stayed with her because he feared that while he had moobs, he wouldn't be able to find anyone else. It certainly looked that way. Helen later discovered he already had a new girlfriend waiting in the wings, so it did all seem to fit. She took all of a morning to feel sorry for herself before throwing herself into work and acting like nothing had ever happened. I suppose I felt bad for her to begin with, until it became apparent that she was up to something quite sinister.

I had made a few good work friends over the past few years. Aside from our team, there was a huge studio full of graphic designers and I had a good friend in that department as well as someone from accounts and a girl in my team. The girl from my team was called Sophia and she was a proper airhead, but hilarious, and I used to love going out for drinks with her after work. We shared a common dislike of Helen and would regularly discuss what a cow she was on our evenings out. Helen had never been one for coming out with us while she had been living with her boyfriend. When she split up with him subtle changes started to happen. It took me a while to notice at first and then it became rather obvious that Helen was coming out on more evenings with us, much to my annoyance.

She then started to invite my friends out with her on the days she knew I couldn't go out. She started to blur the lines and started to invite the girls to her house at weekends. I, of course, was never invited. Slowly but surely, the perception of Helen was that she wasn't such a bad person after all. She was fun, she was crazy, liked to drink and was desperate to get out there and find a boyfriend so used my friends to go out with. The ultimate insult was when she planned a girls holiday to Ibiza and my 'friends' went with her. I was never invited. I could never have been invited. As a rule I was not allowed to be on holiday at the same time as Helen and vice versa, because of the work load. She knew this. She knew exactly what she was doing. I had lost my friends and I knew it.

The subtle way in which Helen took them from me and disguised it as something else, meant that airheads like Sophia didn't really understand the underlying complexities of what I knew Helen was doing. Within time I became upset and started to feel things I had not felt since I was in the playground. I felt hurt and jealous. It was just awful. I hadn't wanted to go back to feeling like this again in my life, ever.

It came to a head while they were all out in Ibiza. My workload had increased anyway as it was a really busy time, but on top of that, a load of adverts that had been booked with Sophia, had not been set we found out at the last minute. It was a massive cock-up. I had to drop everything I was doing in order to set an entire back log of adverts in order to get them to press on time. At about this time I emailed Helen to warn her about what had gone wrong. She was the boss after all. Surely she would want to know this?

I got a phone call from her about an hour later and she told me that the only reason I had told her about anything work related was out of spite because they were in Ibiza and I wasn't. This was meant to be my boss – a responsible, professional manager. I couldn't quite believe it. I put the phone down on her and promptly burst out crying. One of the managers spoke to me and for the first time I told someone everything about how Helen had been treating me.

She returned from Ibiza with two bottles of wine for me and a grovelling apology. What a stupid cow. Finally, the tables turned. She was full of shit. She knew it and now she knew I and everyone else knew it. From that day forward, I pulled her up on everything she did that I knew to be incorrect and unprofessional. If she so much as breathed at me in the wrong way, I took her to task.

I started employing her tactics of saying how I felt in front of the entire team every time she pissed me off. One day she got frustrated over something, forgot herself for a split second and threw a document down at me, swearing loudly. I told her not to behave like that in front of me ever again. She couldn't hack it and asked if she could have a word in our (empty, at the time) MD's office. I gladly went along and as if preordained by the employment satisfaction gods, I ended up taking the MD's chair whilst she sat opposite me like a grovelling little employee.

She told me *I* scared her. It was bizarre. I suppose I just didn't care anymore and she knew it so there was nowhere else she could go with her little bullying trip. She asked for someone else to manage me after that time and they did and I was left alone to do my job like I should have been all along. I didn't stay much longer in the company after this episode. On the plus side, the only good thing to come out of my last few months there was that I met my boyfriend, Ed. We employed him as a designer and we became friends first. He became my rock and the catalyst for me to move on and find something else to get my teeth into, which is what I did.

CHAPTER FIVE

Looking for a new job isn't easy at the best of times, but when you don't even know where you want to work, much less where your skills fit in, it can be quite tricky. Maybe it doesn't matter so much when you are younger as you just think of the pay and the social life you might get out of your next place, but when you get older you start to think about what you actually might like, with a view to staying in the job a bit longer than a year.

Recruitment agencies get a lot of stick from some people. They are sometimes viewed on a par with estate agents in that they are all about sales and not really bothered about your job satisfaction, as long as you interview well, get the job and make them some commission. Some agencies are like that, but some are a little bit better. They take the hassle out of the process of looking for a job. I joined a few agencies on friends' recommendations. Some were good and attentive, some were useless. The last agency I saw was fantastic. Or maybe I just think that because they were the ones who got me a job immediately?

Anyway the fact is that I didn't have a clue what job to go for when I met them. Because I had fallen into my last role without any formal qualifications in marketing or advertising, I didn't really have a clue about the real working world or what jobs I could go for with the small amount of experience I now had in advertising. The qualifications that I did have lay predominantly in acting and the performing arts. It didn't matter to the agency. They realised that with my organisational skills they could be easily transferred to a different role that needed them and it just so happened that on the day I interviewed with them, they were due to see a company who were in need of a PA for their senior property adviser.

PAs basically run people's lives. They do all the tedious things like the paying of bills, collecting of dry cleaning, managing of diaries, arranging appointments and booking of travel and restaurants for high flying people, who simply don't have the time to do it themselves. Even though I had personally never done this for anyone in any previous job, it didn't matter. I simply needed to be highly organised in order to be a PA. If you are organised and have a decent level of common sense, you can be a PA regardless of experience. That's the way they saw it anyway, so they tailored my CV to fit the job and I got an interview which turned into three interviews and then a job offer.

My salary jumped up to £35k and I started working for Greg Broadham in July 2007.

At first being a PA didn't seem so bad at all. On my first day I was shown my office, which was the size of a rabbit hutch. I had to share it with one woman called Amelia who was fifty seven and who had been working for the company for a good few years. Amelia had the best desk opposite the window. My desk was opposite the wall which was rubbish. Aside from working for Greg, I was expected to help another PA called Vera, when she was busy. Vera looked after one of the partners of the company, a man named Adam.

On my first day I found out that Vera had handed her notice in and would be leaving imminently and that another girl had already been found to replace her. I was somewhat disappointed to learn that she would be leaving as she had been the first person to interview me for the job and I recall thinking at the time how hilarious and non-pc she seemed. It was only now that it dawned on me that possibly the reason why she felt able to call the entire company a bunch of inbreds is because she already knew she was leaving. Shame. It would be a month before the new girl arrived and in that time I quickly learned how to be a PA.

There are different types of PAs. You can be a traditional PA which means you do a lot of diary management, meeting arrangements and typing of correspondence. A more modern PA would perhaps not do any typing at all, still look after the boss's diary and book lots of travel. Then you can get the type of PA who does all of the real personal/private stuff like paying of bills, dealing with the wife and children, buying presents, collecting dry cleaning etc.

You also get PAs who are expected to get more involved in the business side of things and attend meetings and take minutes. Greg had me doing a combination of pretty much all of these things so it was a great way to learn. Aside from different types of PA work, you get different types of bosses and not all of them know how to use a PA, or even how to treat them decently. You might think that it wouldn't be that difficult, but some jobs are incredibly difficult for so many different reasons.

Greg was well used to using a PA, which was good for me. However, he was not the easiest of people to work with and so even if I got on with him for the majority of the time, it didn't mean that all those who had come before me or the girls who came after, got on with him. A boss and his PA can have a very close relationship. The level of closeness is determined by the nature of what job the PA has to do. For example, if you are dealing with very sensitive issues and paying of bills or dealing with highly confidential information on a daily basis, then your boss has to be able to trust you on a par with a member of his own family.

As with every relationship you might have in your life, what looks good on paper might not actually work out in practice and, rather like a romantic relationship, there is always a honeymoon period when everything seems to work because everyone is on their best behaviour, trying to give the right impression. There will inevitably come the time though, when the honeymoon phase ends and both boss and PA need to decide if this relationship is one that actually works.

Fortunately for me, Greg decided after a three month probation period that I was good enough for him and I felt the same about him. He was great from the start in that he just gave me tasks to do and left me to get on with them. I had access immediately to his credit and debit card details and was entrusted with them and the purchasing of goods and travel for him. Greg was rarely in the office as he was such a busy and well-respected man. If I saw him once or twice a week it was rare.

I was a true gatekeeper for him. I responded to emails on his behalf, drafted correspondence for him, opened his post, determined what was priority and made sure he knew where he was meant to be and with who and with which board papers, every working day of the week. The only difficult times I encountered with him were on days when he would turn up to the office and just be in a foul mood.

At first it was very difficult trying to understand why he was being so short-tempered and snappy with me. I naturally used to think it was something I must have done to annoy or upset him. I never had the courage to ask though, so instead would put up with it for as long as I could (usually up until lunchtime) and then I would leave the building and call Ed and cry. It was a truly horrid feeling to think that someone just didn't like you. I believe you do have to have a very thick skin to work for some of these high flyers. I know that what I put up with was nothing in comparison to what some PAs put up with and indeed, I would later go on to work for a man who made Greg look like a pussycat, but it still was not easy.

Again, as with a romantic relationship, as soon as the mood had started it would dissolve and you would be none the wiser about what had caused it. It would also be very difficult to hold a grudge because for all of the times I had given him the middle finger from the other side of his office wall because he had pissed me off so much, he would equally be absolutely charming to you and make you feel like the best PA in the world. Eventually I worked him out and learned what buttons not to press and how to compromise and modify my own behaviour and reactions, in order to make the day run as smoothly as possible.

We built up a good working relationship. I read between the lines of his emails when he was tetchy and nine times out of ten would realise that he was in a mood because of his wife, children or a business associate. I did wonder sometimes whether Greg suffered from SMS – Short Man Syndrome. He was not a very tall man and I got the sense that because of this, he sometimes felt the need to prove himself more than others. I don't think it is limited to men though. I once knew a girl who went to a house party with me and summoned me via another friend half way through the evening to go and see her in one of the upstairs bedrooms, where she promptly told me through a flood of tears that it was unfair because I was so tall and she was so small, so boys would never look at her next to me. (She was very drunk and we had both fancied the same person at this particular party, but I had nabbed him first). It was all ridiculous because obviously height has got nothing to do with it!

I am sure it must be worse for a man though as they tend to have bigger egos. Short men seem to be punchier and desperate to make a mark, rather like yappy little dogs. Greg certainly behaved like this on more than one occasion, which was a shame as he really didn't need to be this way. He had enough going for him already. I guess once it's in your psyche though, it's always going to be there. The SMS only ever reared its head occasionally, when Greg felt the need to pull rank if he wasn't getting his own way. Sometimes it was amusing to watch; other times it was irritating, and when he really pissed me off I used to come into the office with four inch heels on and tower over him to get my own back.

On the whole though, I got on with Greg very well. He could be charming, generous and very funny. My colleague Amelia, who I shared the rabbit hutch with, was in a totally different league. She was a big bird; tall, over-bearing, overweight, over-opinionated and bloody annoying. When I had first interviewed with Greg he had mentioned Amelia to me and how she had been through a couple of bereavements and had a few medical issues. He had been politely trying to warn me about her and I started to see why, not long after starting. Amelia was bloody hard work. This might sound harsh because she had been through a very tough time, but I *did* try so very hard to help her and be kind to her. Amelia was a nightmare though and really swung back and forth on the mood pendulum.

At first she was manageable. She helped me understand how Greg could be and I appreciated getting her (incredibly blunt) opinion on some things, work-wise. It helped me get a handle on things. We discovered a mutual love of animals. As time went by we would chat and she seemed okay. She shared with me the tragedies that had happened in her life. Her sister had died tragically just a couple of years back, her parents had died when she was at a young age, one of her brothers was now ill, her first husband had died, her current partner had cancer and she herself had been diagnosed with kidney failure which meant that if a donor could not be found, she faced a life on dialysis. It was all incredibly grim for her and I used to feel so very sorry for her.

As the months went by it became more apparent that the kidney issue was very serious indeed, but Amelia did not want to acknowledge the truth. On a daily basis I never knew what mood she was going to be in when I arrived in the office. Sometimes she was pleasant and cheery and up for having a chat about nice things. Other times I would arrive and say good morning and she wouldn't even acknowledge me so I would know it was a moody day that day.

When her poor long-suffering boss would wander in from his office and cheerily say good morning all he got was 'Is it?'. Some days she cried and I got her a cup of tea and the emergency loo roll for tears. On more than one occasion I would go and up give her a shoulder hug because I felt that she desperately needed a proper one, but she was so very defiant and stubborn that she couldn't quite let it go and I was never quite sure how to deal with the situation any more than I did. In the end she made it incredibly difficult to continue be nice to her because she had a very dark side – a nasty streak. Probably because of all the crap she had been through, granted, but the bottom line was that I was still a work colleague and I had a job to do and my own personal issues to deal with.

My job was incredibly intense and busy. On the days I was overloaded with typing and diary management I really needed peace and quiet to concentrate, but Amelia would not stop talking at me. She was such an overbearing type that I found it difficult to ask her to be quiet if I had work to do. The problem was that she had *no* work to do, at all. It was ridiculous. She would without fail, sit and read the Daily Mail from cover to cover every single day and bark snippets and stories and articles out at me. If she wasn't doing that she would be on the phone to a family member or friend and she had that really annoying habit of raising her voice when on the phone, as though the other person couldn't quite hear her.

I used to turn my dictation machine up to top volume to hear the tapes Greg had left for typing and I was *still* disturbed by her voice. It wound me up to such an extent that I downloaded an app on my phone that measured decibels. When she was on the telephone she reached the 85/90 decibels range and that was sitting at her desk about three metres away. For comparison, a hand drill comes in at 98 db and City traffic comes in at 85 db so you can imagine. It drove me mad.

CHAPTER SIX

Greg took me out for my first Christmas lunch in the December after I had started. He had traditionally always taken Amelia with him too, as her boss wasn't much fun, he felt. So we had gone for lunch at a lovely restaurant in the City at Tower 42. It was all perfectly fine and lovely until the main course, a couple of glasses of champagne in, when the conversation was really flowing. Greg was telling us about how he had been asked to be a trustee of yet another company, but that he dared not tell his wife as she would hit the roof. He was worried that it would involve a heck of a lot more work which would mean less time at home and an unhappy wife. Amelia replied by saying, in all seriousness, through a mouthful of pâté and spitting as she spoke: 'Well, I'm sure you could manage it if you got yourself a decent secretary'.

Hmm. OK. Really hadn't expected that and really wasn't

quite sure how to react, so I just carried on eating, feeling more than a tad awkward at what she had just said. Greg looked equally as uncomfortable as he went slightly red and looked at me for my reaction. It was all incredibly weird, rude and totally uncalled for. That was the thing with Amelia. She was so brazen that she used to come out with things that absolutely floored me. I never knew how to react – not because I literally didn't know what to say, but because this was a work colleague after all and there were meant to be boundaries in the work place, surely?

I came back from a lovely holiday abroad once and had managed to get myself a half-decent tan. Day one back in the office I wore a lemon summer dress with aforementioned tan and the first greeting I got from her was 'Oof! You look like you've been tangoed'. Not, 'How are you? How was your holiday? You look well'. You know the kind of things that most people say to you when you have just returned from a trip abroad.

I swear if I ever said something was black, she would insist it was white. She loved to say controversial things just to wind me up. I presumed she was bored, but also it did smack of jealousy. Here I was, a woman half her age, who was healthy and on the outside seemingly very happy and she had the weight of the world on her shoulders. I get it. I just didn't like it or understand what her motives were for doing it. She was so similar to Helen because she could be nasty, vindictive and snide, but then would buy me gifts for Christmas and my Birthday and put such lovely messages in the cards. It's as though she liked me, but then hated herself for liking me, so reverted back to being obnoxious.

When her partner sadly died due to the cancer that he had, she called me on the weekend in floods of tears. I almost felt honoured that she had chosen me as one of the people she needed to confide in and that perhaps now she would stop the unnecessary needling. She had also been given a lifeline by a family member who donated a kidney to her, so things did seem as though perhaps they might not be so grave after all. I guess at first things did look up. Amelia was chirpier once she got over the sadness of losing her partner, but all too soon she got another boyfriend. Seemingly out of nowhere a chap called Tony appeared in her local village one weekend. (Amelia was lucky enough to have a cottage in the country and a flat in London during the week).

No sooner had she started to get over the grief of losing her last partner, than she started coming in on Mondays with dreadful hangovers as she had been out drinking with Tony. Before long she was coming in to the office mid-week as well, with shocking hangovers because Tony had started to visit her in London. He used to eat all of her food, drink all of her wine and when they were out in the pub, after a heavy session and having put everything on the slate previously, he also had a convenient habit of forgetting his credit card when it came to paying. If that wasn't alarming enough, she also started to be sick from the hangovers when she appeared at work and would be so bad on some days that she had to go home after an hour of arriving in the office.

It was noted by all in the office. This really was not a healthy relationship in any sense. The fact that she was still recovering from having had a kidney transplant, but was getting so drunk she was being sick and bringing her medication back up, was very disturbing. Inevitably with the booze and hangovers, came the foul moods once more.

One day Amelia was asked to actually do some work for a change and it put her in the worst mood ever. She had been down at the photocopier as had Adam's PA, Valerie. When Amelia had finished she marched down the corridor with all the grace of a herd of elephants and immediately launched into an attack on Val. 'Val should really get rid of that mole on her face. It is disgusting. Her life would improve so much if she just got it removed. It is absolutely vile'. It was such a mean and unprovoked attack. There was just no helping Amelia though. I think she was beyond that stage now and I realised that I just couldn't work with her any longer. Every statement that came out of her mouth made me want to scream. I flinched at the mere sound of her voice when she arrived in the mornings. I despised her and everything about her.

*

A good few weeks before I handed in my notice, things got really bad between us and finally led to a row. We had been so close to having a row over the last three and a half years, but both had managed to restrain ourselves before it went too far. She knew she wound me up. I knew she knew. There had often been a horrible unspoken tension between us and it had always been created by her. I was exhausted with it. Tired of feeling like I had to pick up the racket and knock back the jibes, insults and innuendos on a daily basis. She behaved in ways that I would not have entertained in a million years had we been in the real world and that is what used to anger me so much – the fact that if she were just some fat old annoying slob on the street who attempted to speak to me in that way I would have knocked her block off. Inside the office I had to bite my tongue for fear of what would have been unleashed in her direction.

Aside from the drinking, being sick and generally unhealthy living she had been doing with Tony, Amelia had taken to bringing work in that he needed doing, like typing, photocopying and binding. He ran his own business renting out villas to rich clients. She had been working on something when she asked me why she couldn't get into a particular website that Tony had told her about. She asked me quite clearly to look for something with an extension of dot com.

She could not understand why she couldn't get into it. I tried it and each time was told that the web page did not exist. I then tried it with an extension of *.co.uk* and was able to access the website fine. I explained what had happened and instead of being grateful, she went into a complete rage insisting that she had said *.co.uk* all along. I said she had definitely said *.com* which is why I couldn't access it. Again she said she had not, but this time there was an edge to her voice that I hadn't heard before. She was annoyed that I was right and she followed it up with 'I'm not a liar' to which I replied 'Neither am I' and so it continued until I lost it and finally told her exactly what I thought of her.

Nothing was left out. From the excessive volume on the phone, to the mood swings, to her rudeness to me, to the detailed description of how sexy her new boyfriend's balls were – no I am not kidding, she really did tell me one afternoon just how sexy Tony's testicles were. Like I fucking wanted to know what a 60 year old man's balls looked like! I finally told her how she drove me mental and that it was a nightmare to have to share an office with her. And do you know what she had to say to me?

'Well why don't you just fuck off then'.

This said it all, I thought. She had nothing good or constructive to say at all, so all she could revert to was swearing at me pathetically, like a petulant teenager. She was nearly sixty and meant to be educated. God knows how we managed to work together after that, but I think we both knew it was a downhill journey. I still don't think she expected me to hand my notice in though. I don't think anyone did.

CHAPTER SEVEN

I had been putting the feelers out for a while to see what other jobs were out there. The recession had hit whilst I had been employed in my current job and I think everyone who already had a job had been reluctant to give it up, no matter how much they didn't like it. In January 2011, I received a phone call from a recruitment agency telling me about a role that they thought I might like. It sounded like a dream job so I was very excited about it. At this stage they were just finding out whether I wanted to be put forward for it and if so my CV would be sent to the guy I would be working for.

The job was going to be working for the co-founder and MD of a Marketing company in the City as his PA. It would involve a bit of fashion too as he also happened to be the Chairman of a fashion company founded by his girlfriend. I was asked if I had any interest in fashion, which I did. I had collected Vogue magazine since the age of thirteen and had religiously collected every single British edition of it between 1991 and 2001, plus many more British and International issues since. I was asked if I wanted to be considered. I told them I was very keen and I waited impatiently for the call to say I had been chosen to interview.

On a chilly January evening at 6.30pm I arrived at the offices of the fashion company for my interview with Rich Donaldson. I was guided into a showroom that had his girlfriend's new collection hanging up all around me, highlighted by tiny ceiling spotlights. Fur garments and silk dresses adorned with diamante, floated perfectly in harmony with each other, oozing with elegance and expensiveness. I felt giddy to think I was here.

The designer in question was someone I had definitely heard of. I was thrilled to think a job could be mine working with someone so closely connected to this world. It seemed far more glamorous than the world of property that I had been working in for the past nine years. The door handle turned and in walked Rich. I already knew what he looked like as had seen pictures of him and his girlfriend, and had thought what a handsome couple they were.

In the flesh he was even more attractive. Tall, well built, dressed impeccably and with a deep tan. Not the off-putting perma-tan sported by some old school Hollywood legends, but the type gained from constant hopping to the South of France for a few days here and there.

Rich was charming. I bought it completely. I genuinely thought what a warm, well mannered, well-spoken man he was. We spoke about my experience. He flattered me. Told me I had an amazing CV and that he had been sent a bunch by the agency, but he had immediately binned all but two of them because they were not up to the standard he required. I was one of the two he had kept and he made it clear that he would be seeing no more. So, already I knew I was down to the last two candidates for the job. Inside I was beyond giddy.

And then the girlfriend herself arrived. She was uber attractive. Packaged incredibly and wearing one of her own designs, with her nails perfectly polished and her long, dark, glossy hair swaying. She greeted Rich first with a 'Hello darling' and a kiss. Sexual electricity flowed between them. She then shook my hand. I warmed to her immediately. I had never wanted a job more than I wanted this one.

They both proceeded to gush over me and my experience and told me in detail what kind of work they wanted me for. It turned out that Rich had never had a PA to himself, having only ever shared one with two other people. He really wanted one now to deal with his personal life – paying of bills, dealing with staff at his home and on board his yacht which was moored in France. The idea was that he could then concentrate on winning more business for the firm he had started with his business partner. I was told that two days a week I would get to travel to the fashion offices to help out with administration and events planning.

It all sounded a dream. I was desperate to sign on the dotted line. I left the interview on a complete high from a mixture of having met someone famous and with the prospect of working in a really exciting world. I felt I deserved it. It was right that I should be moving into this stratosphere finally.

The next day I got feedback from the agency that I had gone down well and that the warmth I had felt from them, had been reciprocated. They still wouldn't be pinned down on a date for a second interview, but what I heard was good enough for me. Or so I thought.

I had never been in a situation where I had ever waited too long to hear about a job before. I was about to find out what it felt like though.

When you are half way out the door of one job, you suddenly cannot think of anything else apart from leaving. It becomes an unhealthy obsession. Every task that you once did on a daily basis suddenly becomes the most tedious thing in the world, ever. The very action of dragging yourself to your office every day becomes a chore.

On top of that, if you are actually waiting on news of a job offer or of a second interview it can be doubly cruel. I would have rather stayed at home watching daytime TV than go into my office with Amelia, every day that I was left waiting for news. It was tortuous. Respite came only on the weekend because I could amuse my mind with activities rather than wonder why I had not heard back from the effervescent Rich.

I started to Google 'waiting to hear back after a job interview' on a half hourly basis, scanning the various forums that existed, written by other desperate job seekers. It drove me to distraction. Looking for a job is exactly like dating. The same emotions are involved.

JOB SEEKING	DATING
Meet potential new boss.	Meet potential new partner.
Have a great connection.	Have a great connection.
Leave the encounter on a high, having been told they will be in touch soon.	Leave the encounter on a high, having been told they will call you.
The next day you are in the afterglow, replaying all the good bits.	The next day you are in the afterglow, replaying all the good bits.
By next day you have heard nothing and doubt starts to creep in. You keep checking your phone to see if they have called. By 4pm you reset your phone thinking there must be a problem with it.	By next day you have heard nothing and doubt starts to creep in. You keep checking your phone to see if they have called. By 4pm you reset your phone thinking there must be a problem with it.
You get to the next day with no word still. You start to think really shitty things about them like they weren't all that anyway and do I really want to work for someone who can't be bothered to get in touch? I'm better than that company anyway. I didn't like the receptionist when I arrived anyway.	You get to the next day with no word still. You start to think really shitty things about them like they weren't all that anyway and do I really want to go out with someone who can't be bothered to get in touch? They weren't that good looking. They probably have really bad personal habits.
Day four and you are seriously angry. You send an e-mail in to the agency to see if they have had any feedback. You start asking friends what it might mean and get confused by the differing opinions on why after four days you haven't heard back. 'If you haven't heard back after day one then they aren't interested in you.' 'No news is good news. They are probably just going through the motions of interviewing others as a necessity before giving you an offer.'	Day four and you are seriously angry. You send an e-mail in to your friends asking them for advice. You get confused by the differing opinions on why after four days you haven't heard back. 'If you haven't heard back after day one then they aren't interested that you.' 'No news is good news. They are probably just trying to play it cool before asking you out on another date.'

You can probably imagine how frustrated I was when, after two weeks I still hadn't heard anything apart from 'you are the favoured candidate still'. I couldn't have given a toss if I was – what I wanted was a cold, hard, job offer, or confirmation of a second interview. Anything, just to make me feel like there was hope and a chance of escaping the rabbit hutch! I finally got a call to confirm that I had been asked to go back for another interview with Rich, at his offices in the City. It was set for the next week and my mood improved dramatically.

I arrived at the City offices suited and raring to go. I was not disappointed in what I found. One of the highest buildings I had ever been in and the offices where Rich was based were on the 30th floor. The speed of the lift was insane. I was told that it was the second speediest lift in Europe. I think it took all of seven seconds to reach the dizzying heights of D&D Associates. The view looking over London was breath-taking. I was shown into a floor to ceiling, glass fronted boardroom where I sat and waited for Rich. He appeared in another stunning suit, all blue eyes and tan with a huge smile on his face. The job was mine, I could feel it. I didn't even see the need for the second interview, but told myself he probably just needed to go through the motions if there was indeed a second candidate being considered.

We chatted casually for a while. There wasn't really much to say though. I recall him mentioning the current PA and that he thought she would probably not stay on with them for much longer and that if that was the case I might have to do a small percentage of work for his business partner Dick Dinage. I was so keen on just getting the job offer that I didn't read much into any of this, but I really should have as I was later to discover. Rich showed me around the offices and where I would be sitting. I was happy. We shook hands and I left.

As with the first interview, I was happy for at least the first day afterwards but, when I still had not had a call or an email from the agency, I again became restless. I called them and asked if they had heard anything. They had heard nothing but agreed to call Rich on my behalf. I heard nothing again until just before the end of the day, when they finally called me.

My heart started to race as I saw the call on my phone. I managed to pick it up and walk gingerly out of the office and into Greg's office, which was empty as he was away on business. I quietly closed his office door and answered the call in a semi-whisper. My heart righted itself almost immediately when I heard the words 'Hi, we just wanted to update you on the latest, which is we haven't heard back from Rich yet, but we will try him again tomorrow'.

For god's sake! I thought. What was wrong with him? Why couldn't he just tell them the job was mine and put me out of my misery? I did not understand what the hold-up could be. Over the next three days I waited and wondered and fumed. Some nights I got home and was so frustrated with the whole situation that I burst into tears, because I was so close yet so far.

Red wine became my saviour and the only thing able to send me into a sleep; otherwise I would have spent half of the night going over the two interviews in my head, bit by bit. Finally the next day I got a phone call from the agency saying that the job was mine. I was relieved, yet totally underwhelmed, which is not the way I had felt before when offered a job. The exact words that Rich had uttered were, apparently, 'Yeah, let's do this'. I had waited and wondered and been driven mad for the last four weeks and so the finale ended up being a damp squib.

I asked the agency what the final salary was going to be. I

was told £38,000. This was even less than I was earning at my current job. I had been told all along that although he would only offer that to begin with, he was aware that I wanted more and that they would be prepared to increase after a three month probation period. I asked the agency about this. I said that I would be happy to accept if it was written into my contract that my salary would be reviewed after three months. The agency said they would call me back.

They called me back within about twenty minutes. All was not well. Apparently my request for this to be written into my contract had not gone down well at all with Rich. According to the agency he was most upset that I would even dream of asking for this. So now all of a sudden I was the bad guy. I could not have felt worse. The agency had told me all along that this would be OK and now because I had requested it and it had made Rich angry, they were backing off from ownership of the idea.

I felt sick to the stomach and scared. Scared of the can of worms I had opened. Scared that I wasn't going to get the job after all and, even if I did, that he would think I was just a money-grabbing bitch. I made a decision to call him directly. I got his phone number from the company website.

He answered in his usual charming way. I said it was me. His mood darkened. I tried to explain as much as I could about the situation. I thought if we could talk, he would lighten up and remember what a great candidate I was and agree to increase my salary after three months. How wrong I was. It was awful. Just a hideously uncomfortable conversation to have to have with someone I was potentially about to start working for. Talk about starting off on the wrong foot.

Apart from his anger I recall one major thing from our brief conversation. I remember him clearly saying that he knew what secretaries were worth and it wasn't going to be more than £38,000. We ended our chat with him telling me to have a think about it. The offer was there and I could take it or leave it. I honestly wanted to be sick. Part of me wanted to tell Rich and his massive ego to go fuck himself. I now knew from our conversation that he was an arsehole. Who quibbles over the sake of £2k for the right candidate? Who gets a weed on about even being asked to increase an offer by £2k? Surely he knew this was how business went? Of course he knew, he was just being a tosser for the sake of it.

On the other hand though, my mind started playing games on me. Maybe I was being unreasonable. Maybe I wasn't worth more than this. Maybe I should be grateful to work for him and surely all of the perks would make up for it all? I went back to my desk in turmoil and found that the agency had already emailed a copy of the contract to me. I looked at it. I saw my basic salary in black and white. I then saw that I would get a clothing allowance of £2k per year that had to be spent on his girlfriend's fashions. I also noted that there was a bonus scheme in place. I convinced myself that this might not be so bad after all and with the fear of having to stay on in my current role, with grumpy Amelia barking at me on a daily basis, I accepted it.

From having been hesitant, I was suddenly chomping at

the bit, rather foolishly. I should have given it some time to think and asked a few people their opinions. I may have felt differently after a night's sleep, but instead I rushed in like an idiot. Rich's tactics had worked. He had treated me badly, disrespected me and my profession and here I was desperate to take his job offer, at a salary lower than I was currently on and all because I couldn't wait to escape my current job.

If I thought that this part had all been a bit insulting, the best was yet to come; because instead of Rich being pleased that I was willing to accept his offer, he gave me the silent treatment. It just smacked of game playing and I did not like it one bit.

The agency had passed my acceptance on to him. I have no doubt that in the modern world even if he had been out at meetings all day, he would have seen this on his Blackberry. He was choosing to punish me by making me sweat, because I dared to request more money. I should have called it quits then and told him to stuff his poxy job. Looking back now I wish I had, because it is certainly what my gut was telling me to do. Like a fool though, I thought of the trappings. I was more interested in being able to say that I looked after his girlfriend in some capacity.

I'll admit that for someone who dreamt of fame and fortune as a young girl, the next best thing sometimes was the connection to a famous person. You can hang off the coat tails and show off to people as you name drop, but I learned that it doesn't work like this and it is pretty sad to think like this. I wish I had had more conviction at this stage in my life.

I suppose it was all part of the learning process of my life and this was just one part that would lead me to a higher path and a greater understanding of myself, which ultimately would be the best thing for me.

I was still waiting for any kind of response by the afternoon of the next day. I felt desperate and took matters into my own hands. I composed an email to Rich pointing out how much warmth I had felt from him on our first meeting and how honoured I would be to work for him. In short, I sucked up to him majorly, as I thought this is what the fucker wanted. It sickened me to do it, but I had made my mind up that I absolutely wanted this job and wanted out of my current one. Rich made me wait until the end of the day, when he finally replied with a one liner to my gushing email.

'Hmmm. I'll have a think. Let me revert' was his reply.

I could not bloody believe it. I was absolutely fuming. Have a think? Have a fucking think about what? You have already offered me the job, you dick! All that has happened in the interim period is I have tried to negotiate for a bit more money, because guess what? I think I'm worth it. It's not like its unheard of either, is it? Most people with any self-worth will ask for an improvement on what the initial salary offer is.

I was being made to wait yet again. He knew exactly what he was doing. It was obvious he was a game-player and a control freak. I went home that evening utterly despondent. I drank a vat of red wine and came so close to sending an email to Rich, telling him to go and screw himself and to this day,

I wish that I had. How I resisted venting my venom at him, I really don't know.

I had to wait another whole day before I heard anything further from Rich. I had no idea what was happening. The agency was at a loss and could not get anything from him and had now turned into pussies themselves, because they kept saying they didn't want to hassle him in case it angered him further. It was the most ridiculous situation. I heard back from Rich finally. His moody disposition had been replaced with the joys of spring.

He was asking if I would be prepared to go and meet his business partner and co-founder of the company, Dick Dinage. It turned out that the reason for the waiting was because the old PA had indeed left the company and now it looked like I would be doing more work for Dick than previously anticipated. I was so pissed off that it was still on-going. Thank god I hadn't handed my notice in yet. I reluctantly agreed to meet with this Dick character.

I was supposed to meet Dick Dinage at the offices on the 30th floor. Instead he waited for me in the lobby and suggested we go for a coffee nearby. It all seemed a bit cloak and dagger. Dick was a scary looking chap. He was overweight with a ruddy complexion (no doubt from excessive boozing) and had the oddest eyes I had ever seen. He had a way of staring at you with his head tipped down towards you, which made him look like a serial killer. I didn't like him. I found him very strange indeed and the conversation did not flow. I spent twenty minutes with him and left. The most ironic thing about meeting him was that he at least sent me an email later that evening saying 'Welcome to D&D'! Which is more than I ever received from Rich. From this, I gathered that the job was still mine.

I got the agency to confirm the next day that I could finally hand my notice in, which they did. I felt relieved, but not ecstatic as you would hope to feel, which was disappointing to say the least. It had taken six weeks exactly from the first interview to get to this stage which was quite depressing and completely took the shine off it all.

I worked my notice which was a month less any holiday I was owed, which I was allowed to use in order to shorten my notice. Greg, my boss was not happy. He knew deep down though that I could not work with Amelia any longer and made no noises about wanting me to stay. I found a replacement for me and my last day came about very quickly. Amelia gave me a gift and a card. The card was full of love and kisses. Her gift however was a Clarins face mask, created especially for women with hormonal imbalances. The message was not lost on me. What a bitter and twisted, vindictive old sour puss she was. I was well out of there, or so I thought.

CHAPTER EIGHT

I started work at D&D Associates in March 2011. I arrived on the 30th Floor and Rich came to collect me from reception. He was back to his charming self and made me feel very welcome indeed. He walked me round the office and introduced me to all other members of staff. Unfortunately the office Manager, Ali, was not in that day as she had taken part in the London Marathon over the weekend and was recovering. Otherwise she would have shown me the ropes. I was assured that I would be shown everything the day after though.

So, in the interim period I sat at my desk and logged in. I had started at 8.30am. It was now 9am. There was a guy who sat opposite me normally, but he only ever came into the office on Tuesdays, Wednesdays and Fridays so he wasn't there on my first day either. The whole office was open plan. Rich and Dick sat opposite each other across huge desks and had chosen not to have their own private offices. Instead they mucked in with everyone else on the floor, maintaining that it was because they wished to have an open door policy.

Except it became apparent over time that actually it was only because Rich was super paranoid and needed to hear everything that went on in the office. Their desks were to my left. We were separated by a mere three metres of carpet. Dick wasn't there on my first day either. So just Rich and I sat there in total silence for what felt like an age.

I was used to working with Greg who had given me tasks to do and kept me busy. It appeared that Rich didn't actually have anything for me to do. I honestly did not know what to do with myself. My computer screen faced the main part of the office which was behind me and as I was closest to the main entrance to the floor and the toilets, there was always someone who could see my screen so I felt I could do nothing but look at the company's website. I had to pretend to be busy for at least three hours. All that time Rich sat there in silence, tapping away at his PC or on the telephone.

He didn't talk to me, ask me for anything or offer any insight into what I was supposed to do for the next five and a half hours. I was already starting to wonder what the hell I had taken on. It was pure torment.

Rich had this brooding presence that made you feel like you couldn't even ask a question, let alone for any work to be getting on with. His demeanour always suggested that he was deep in concentration and therefore did not want to be disturbed. You got the impression that if you were to disturb him, he'd rip your head off so I decided to stay silent and pretend to be busy, which was just fucking ridiculous.

On day two things improved by a slight margin. Ali, the office manager was back. She hobbled towards me with her John Wayne post-marathon legs to say hello. She was nice, but didn't seem too enthused about the company or any work I might have to do. She did tell me that I had replaced a girl who had previously looked after three people (Rich, Dick and a feisty female director, called Bernadette). A second PA had been employed to look after Bernadette solely, so now no one knew exactly what work I would actually have to do. In fact, the previous PA's time had mostly been taken up with Bernadette and her demanding ways.

It was looking more and more likely that my job was not one that would keep me busy. I was starting to worry again. For the rest of that particular day I browsed the company website another few hundred times in between going to the kitchen to make cups of tea (which also meant that thankfully, every so often I would have to travel to the ladies, which was a genuine highlight of my day). I appreciated anything that broke up the monotony of just sitting there, hour after hour with Rich's ever present form hovering to my left. I was scheduled to attend a few training sessions that week, but apart from that, there really wasn't much else I could be getting on with. My colleague Mike had arrived back in the office by now though at least. He was incredibly friendly and made me feel very much at home. I was grateful just to have someone to talk to which killed the boredom of waiting for any work to actually be thrown my way.

I started to sense that Rich probably didn't like us talking much though. He used to look over at us with a puzzled look on his face and would often make comments about how he had never heard Mike laugh before and this would embarrass Mike. Rich would always say things with a smile on his face, but I knew that he really meant 'shut the fuck up. No one should be having fun in my office – least of all you two'. It was quite an oppressive atmosphere.

I think for the remainder of my week I was asked to do a total of two things for Rich – book him a taxi and sort out a paper jam in his printer. I was bored beyond belief and when the weekend arrived it could not have come any sooner.

I honestly thought that things would improve on the work front and that perhaps this was just the teething stage where Rich wasn't quite sure what project to throw my way first. Either that or perhaps I had joined at a particularly busy period for him where he simply didn't have the time to sit down and go through anything with me. I made do with the scraps of work that I was given and on the days that Mike was in, I was at least able to have a chat with him.

The one thing that I did start doing was going to get Rich his lunch on a daily basis. It was something I actually looked forward to, as it at least got me out of the office. He had the same lunch every single day – six California rolls and a strawberry and banana smoothie from the Sushi place nearby. He never varied what he ate or drank. I used to get a free portion of edamame beans and a Diet Coke because of a meal deal that was in place. I used to keep the Diet Coke for myself and give Rich the beans, which he always gave back to me to have instead.

A perk of working in such a great building was that there was a stunning gym that was housed in the basement. It was probably the best gym I had ever seen – all fluffy towels and free robes, shower products and hair care, plus a trouser press and hairdryers and straightening irons. Our company paid for two roaming gym cards for us all to use. The deal was that every day there were eight slots available. Two people could go at 7.30 to 8.30am, 12.30 to 1.30pm, 1.30 to 2.30pm and 6.30pm onwards.

Twice a week, I used the card on the 1.30 to 2.30pm slot and swam in the 25 metre pool. In the full hour, I had time to swim and then go to the 'chill-out room', which was dedicated to just relaxing. It was a darkened room with massage chairs and blankets and a huge fish tank, where stressed out and hung over City folk could go for a sleep, to recharge their batteries. I used to have twenty minutes in there and then go and shower, using the luxury products that were available free of charge. On these two days of the week, at least my day never seemed to be that bad. Going on the later session meant that once I came back to my desk at 2.30pm, I only ever had three hours to go before home time. The rest of my days and weeks used to drag though.

It might sound like another person's pleasure, being paid

to sit at a desk in stunning offices, doing absolutely nothing, but to me it was pure pain. Pure pain made even worse by the fact that Rich sat there day in day out, in my peripheral vision. It was like some weird game where he knew that I had absolutely no work to do and I knew he knew and I felt like some big fake. I felt a huge amount of guilt that all I was doing was looking at Google, Facebook and the Daily Mail showbiz section, on an hourly basis. He must have known. He also must have known what it was doing to me – i.e. driving me a bit mental.

Dick had been an irregular face in my first few weeks of work. Rumour had it, that he had been to a very expensive clinic in Switzerland to try and lose his excess rolls of fat, via some plastic tubes. It was typical of him to pay to lose the weight whilst he sat on his fat arse, rather than actually put the effort in and do some exercise.

I hadn't really had much contact with him at all and I had taken quite a few phone calls for him on the days he was out. I took a call one afternoon from a fast spoken chap who called himself Roger. He had called Dick's direct line and I had intercepted the call. All he had asked was if Dick was there and when I said no, he asked if he would call him back so I asked for a name and a telephone number.

As always, I asked if Dick would know what the call was about, to which Roger had replied 'Oh yes, he knows me'. Now I don't know about you, but I wasn't about to start questioning someone who claimed to know the co-owner of the company, just in case this Roger chap was a hugely important person and just in case I ended up offending him and getting myself into a whole lot of bother with Dick, so I left it at that. I sent an email to Dick with the subject of 'Telephone Message' and explained who had called, in the main body of the email. I thought no more of it once I had pressed send.

In the few weeks I had been at D&D, I had made a fair few friends. It so happened that even though I was new, a few girls on the support side had only been there a month or so longer than me also, so they were all keen to get a social life started, which I wasn't complaining about. My friend from outside of work was attending a gig that night where her boyfriend's band was playing. I had invited a couple of the girls from work.

The gig wasn't due to start until about 9pm so as soon as 5.30pm hit, we all piled down to the bar near the office and started the night off there. It was in the cab on the way to the gig, that I felt my bag buzzing away and knew it was my work Blackberry. I foraged around until I found it and then looked at it just as we pulled up to the venue.

It was an email from Dick. The subject read 'That was Shite'. I wasn't quite sure what to think, but immediately opened it and read down until I reached the end, convinced that the email had been sent in error to me or that the way it had been worded made me think that Dick had forwarded something to me from someone else and perhaps I had to figure out what I was meant to do with it. It was usually the case that bosses would send me emails with not much instruction and it was down to me to read the whole thing and piece together the clues, to decide what they actually wanted me to do with it. I think I re-read the email twice more before it finally dawned on me that this vile, rude and altogether unnecessary email had in fact actually been meant for me all along.

My heart started to race. Dick had replied to my earlier telephone message to him and had actively changed the subject from 'Telephone Message' to 'That was shite'. He had then continued to say how he had called 'Roger' back and that I 'obviously hadn't', because he had been forced to listen to fifteen minutes of 'fucking waffle'. He said that I should have taken more information from him and that the whole thing was sloppy and totally unlike me (because apparently Dick knew me). He had typed this at 8pm.

I was shocked. I don't think I had ever been sent such a horrible or unfair email. My first instinct was to reply straight away to him and say 'You fucking what?' because I was so angry. Instead I decided to forward his email along with my original one, to Rich. I said 'Please see below. I do not appreciate having to read emails like this, nor do I expect to have to do so'. Then my rage turned into tears.

I felt utterly wretched. Someone who barely knew me had basically decided that I was rubbish and had told me in no uncertain terms. I wanted to punch his lights out, the fat bastard. I continued with my evening and ended up getting drunk; more so than I would normally on a school night. I went into rebellious mode and no longer cared about whether I went into work the next day or not. I knew I was rebelling. I was fed up of being treated unfairly in every job I had and I needed to demonstrate how this had made me feel. I decided I was going to be unreliable. If you always try your best and work really hard and you still get grief, what more can you do apart from walk out of the job? As I certainly could not afford to walk away from any job, I decided to be awkward instead. The fat sod wasn't going to get away with speaking to me like that.

The next day I woke up early with a huge hangover and felt morose about the situation having happened at all. I sent an email to Rich saying I had a headache and I would not be in until later that day. I got a response back saying he would sort Dick out, but played the guilt card about how he really needed me in the office, as there was a really important meeting he wanted me to be part of.

He was clever. He knew exactly how to reel me in. He knew that thus far I had been given no work of any gravity at all. He also knew that there was a real danger of me telling them all to get lost after Dick's highly unpleasant email, so he had decided to tempt me with the prospect of actually being involved in some proper work stuff, finally. Using the age old 'I really need you' thing also suckered me in. So, I got dressed, took some painkillers and made my way in.

CHAPTER NINE

I had access to both Dick and Rich's emails. As soon as I got into the office, I decided to look at the outgoing ones that Dick had sent the night before. I saw an email that he had sent to a personal friend just after he had sent me mine. It read 'On the Claret again. Oops'! So now I knew. Dick had fallen off the wagon and had plunged head first into a vat of red and Mr Nasty had appeared; not that I was excusing his behaviour. I also saw an email that Rich had sent to him, tearing a strip off him for sending me such an email, so for a while I thought that Rich actually had my back.

I had my first meeting with Rich and two other account managers about a potential new client and finally felt part of the company. Half way through the meeting, Rich winked at me as if to cement the whole 'we are part of a team and I need you'. He really was great at his job, I was beginning to learn.

Bullshitting and schmoozing really was part of his blood. Like a fool, I bought it.

When Dick finally appeared in the office two days later, having been away at his detox clinic, he walked towards his desk with a sheepish smile on his face. He knew he'd been a drunken arse. I smiled back with pursed lips and nothing was said. The days ticked along and everybody had forgotten the email incident, or so I thought.

One morning a couple of weeks later, Dick had called across to me asking me to book him an appointment that lunchtime with 'George'. I had absolutely no clue as to who George was. I asked and Dick told me he would be in his contacts, under osteopathy. So I started to look on my PC. Dick left for a meeting soon after and as I was about to call to make Dick's appointment, I heard Rich muttering about something under his breath. I looked across at him and at first he didn't say anything and then after a while he looked over at me and started to talk. I couldn't decipher what he was saying because he was almost whispering it, but it was definitely aimed at me. I heard something about him being 'fucking angry' so I said 'Sorry?' and he whispered some more unintelligible stuff again, so I was forced to get up from my desk and walk across to him. I only realised on approaching him that he was full of rage. I don't think I had ever seen him look like this before, although I imagine that he looked pretty similar to this on the day I had asked about my salary being increased.

What he said next was so off the wall, I struggled to

understand what on earth he was banging on about, but I gathered that his beef was with Dick. He said he was 'fucking livid' that Dick had asked me to book a hairdressing appointment and that I had not been employed to do 'shit' tasks like that for him. I was slightly confused over the mention of a hairdresser and asked what he meant. I then explained that George was an osteopath to which Rich raised an eyebrow and said 'And you believe that shit?' He was really aggressive and I was feeling more uncomfortable by the second.

I just wanted the bizarre conversation to be over, but Rich clearly had a bee in his bonnet so felt compelled to come out with some further nonsense. He asked me if I knew about the Stockholm syndrome. I had heard of it and knew what it meant, but I literally could not comprehend what this had to do with me booking an osteopath appointment for Dick. Rich's fury increased, but with it his voice became more quiet and menacing. He started to talk about the incident over the email that had happened two weeks prior and I realised what the connection was with the Stockholm syndrome. Clearly Dick was the captor in this warped scenario and I was the hostage, because if I was willing to book appointments for Dick then that clearly meant that I liked Dick sending me nasty emails. Yeah, I didn't get where this was coming from either, but this was really happening. Rich then went on to say 'I don't want to have to find myself a new PA in six months' time, because the one I hired is not doing any of the tasks I want, but rather booking hair appointments and other shite tasks for Dick'.

I was stunned with the way Rich was speaking to me. It was so unpleasant. I was damned if I did and damned if I didn't, and it was a hideous position to be put in. There was literally nothing I could say to Rich. It was like he was possessed. I walked back to my desk and my eyes started to fill with tears. I held them back but Mike noticed and asked if I was OK. I emailed him asking if I could have a chat with him later on. I couldn't believe that for the second time in as many weeks the other boss was now turning psycho on me. I went swimming that lunch time and the pool had been practically empty. I swam harder and harder and got angrier with each length that I did.

Rich was so strange and because none of what he had said had made any real sense, it had been impossible to have a rational conversation about it, which left me feeling utterly frustrated and helpless, which in turn made me furious. I made the decision to go and talk to him after lunch; to nip this in the bud like I had with the Dick/email situation.

I had arranged to meet Mike first in the lobby downstairs. Mike felt bad for me and could not understand why Rich had been so strange with me. He did give me a little more insight into the dynamics of Rich's relationship with Dick though. It was strained to say the least. They had been in business for a while and it was almost like a bad marriage – they loved each other, but despised certain things about each other. Rich thought Dick was lazy and Dick thought Rich was a nag. Rich was a complete health freak, Dick was an overweight alcoholic. Mike agreed that I should speak to Rich directly if it had upset me so much.

I took the lift to our floor and the doors opened at reception. I asked the reception girls if Rich had come back from his lunch yet. Just as they were trying to recall whether he had or hadn't, the other lift door opened and out he stepped. He looked suspicious as soon as he saw me, smiled and asked if everything was OK. I said no. Reflex reaction. There was no time like the present.

I gulped and asked if I could have a word and then guided him into a nearby meeting room. He asked if I was upset as my face visibly crumpled as soon as we were behind closed doors. I was nervous, but most of all I was still upset at how he had spoken to me earlier. I nodded as I suddenly could not speak. 'Have I upset you?' he asked and I nodded again and tried to stop the tears. I was determined to talk to him in a professional manner and not let these bloody tears get in the way again.

He looked genuinely disappointed. Said he was sorry he had upset me and that it was not his intention. I said I found it odd that he had talked about the Stockholm syndrome scenario. He tried his best to get out of it and make it all seem very jokey, but I wasn't buying any of it. He tried to explain what he had meant and said that he was genuinely annoyed if Dick was going to start asking me to do menial tasks, because at the very moment he might need me, he was worried that I would be snarled up in another project for Dick. I told him that if I was meant to work some of the time for Dick then what else was I supposed to do when he asked me to do something for him – say no? He said yes that I was supposed to refuse and say I was busy with something else. I refused and explained that for a PA it was incredibly difficult to say no to someone who was the co-founder of the business and that if he really didn't want me working for him on certain things or at certain parts of the day, he needed to have that talk with Dick, not me.

It was utterly preposterous that it should fall on me to do Rich's dirty work for him. I felt pretty miserable for the rest of that day and I suspected that nothing much would change at all, despite our chat. I was right. The weeks went by and nothing changed at all.

CHAPTER TEN

I had known from when I started at D&D that the glorious spot at the top of the skyscraper was not a permanent thing. Apparently one of the top directors of the holding company did not like heights and had asked for the company to be moved to a lower floor. We were due to move at the end of May and the move date had snuck up on us all. Everyone was responsible for packing their own stuff into a crate that would then be moved along with your PC and phone to a new office on the 9th floor. I wasn't looking forward to it as I would seriously miss the dizzying heights we were all used to. From our current view point you could see weather changing before it hit the ground. Clouds used to float past our windows that you could have touched, they were that close. From the 9th floor, however, the view was particularly uninspiring.

The move took place over a weekend, helped by key members of staff. I arrived at the 9th floor at my usual time of 8.30am the next Monday, to find everything in its place as it had been upstairs, but now on a lower level with nothing much to look at apart from the Barbican centre in all its concrete glory. Rich and Dick were already in the office when I arrived. I had thought I would have a pretty normal day, but Rich had other ideas.

The office move had spurred him into action and he seemed manic. He kept shouting across at me requesting new things, like foliage, as it was now too bare near his desk. He asked me look into getting a privacy shield for his computer screen and then gave me orders about getting him fruit in the mornings. All pointless bollocks, to make himself look important. Then he walked over to the area that was near to my desk. Instead of me being near to the toilets, I was now closest to the stationery and binding area. I also noted that the girl I was most friendly with in the office, had been moved completely away from me and out of my line of vision, which I know had been deliberately planned by Rich.

Rich approached me and motioned towards the stationery area. He said that I had to start policing the area and ensuring that people kept it neat and tidy. It was now my responsibility. He then turned very conspiratorial indeed and lowered his voice while he said 'You've played it very well up until now. People genuinely like you, which I think is brilliant because you've got them on side. I now think it's time to pull back a bit though. I need you to totally police this area of the office including mine and Dick's desks. We have a lot of sensitive information on and around our desks'.

It all made sense now as to why my friends had been moved away from me. The only person close to me aside from the bosses was Mike and Mike of course, was only in the office three times a week. Whereas my friends used to walk by my desk and say hello, I now got the distinct impression that they were not welcome. I began to get worried if they came close as I could feel Rich's eyes burning into me. I had to start shooing people away from me if they ever stopped to talk. I felt like I was in solitary confinement and was not allowed to speak with anyone. There had been a definite shift from us being on the upper floor, to the lower.

As my world became more and more isolated, my work load became less and less. I was starting to go a little bit mad. My days started fine due to the fact that in the mornings I had had a whole night's sleep to help me forget the previous day, but by 9am each day I had already looked at my personal emails, the Daily Mail website and Facebook and was bored. Every day Rich would be sat to my left, silent and brooding. I was still being given no work. My only moments of freedom came when I went to the loo, made either myself or Rich a cup of tea or went at 12.30pm sharp to collect Rich's lunch. Unfortunately Rich decided in early June that he was going to start mixing his diet up a little so decided he no longer wanted sushi. I would therefore not be required to go to collect it for him. I now had one less thing to do during my day.

I was so depressed. I felt miserable and exhausted with it.

As soon as 5.30pm arrived each day I wanted to leave, but I knew that even that was frowned upon. I used to have to sit there spinning out the last twenty minutes or so until I could get as near to 6pm as I could possibly bear, before summoning the courage up to ask if I could leave. I felt like an absolute fool asking if there was anything else I could do for Rich, considering I had done absolutely nothing for him all day anyway, but ask I did.

I would then gather my coat and bag and head for the door. By the time I reached my front door at home I felt utterly spent and regularly used to get inside my flat, close the door and cry, just to relieve my frustration. I am sure that from the outside it sounds like a complete doss to some. Go to work, do nothing, get paid, go home. It was far from this. Rich was a control freak. He simply wanted a being to sit near to him at all times when he was in the office, ready to jump when he decided he had a scrap of work for you. He had moved my friends away from me. He didn't like me being too friendly with anyone else in the office, he didn't want anyone approaching me at my desk and I wasn't allowed to leave on time. I felt trapped. He wanted to control me, but the very nature of trying to battle against succumbing to this, on a daily basis, was taking its toll on me.

When I started at D&D, I knew I was on a three month probationary period. I was well aware that the three month period was up soon, but nothing had been mentioned by Rich, so I presumed that I would simply pass it and would get a letter telling me so. One Friday just before lunch I realised that on the following Monday the three months would be up. Rich had been in a particularly buoyant mood that morning, so as I headed out for lunch and asked him if there was anything I could get for him, I foolishly decided to also casually mention the matter of probation. I guess I was fishing for info on what would happen next – would I get a letter or have a chat with him and/or even a pay rise? I had not been expecting what he said next. Oh, so very casually, Rich said 'Yes about that, I've been meaning to say. I think I'm going to extend it'.

I don't think my jaw dropped quite fully open. I think I said 'Oh' and before I could say anything else, he continued with his monologue. 'Yeah the thing is that you haven't actually done any of the things that I employed you to do, so until that has happened I can't really judge anything and I have no idea that when you *do* start doing these things, that you will even like doing them, so this gives you an opportunity to back out if you don't like the job after all'. He said it so bloody breezily, like it was nothing. I wanted to vomit on him.

What a fucking cock. What an utter crock of shit he had just fed me. As if it was *my* fault that *he* hadn't managed to get off *his* arse and actually work out what he wanted from me in three months he had already had me at his beck and call. As if it was just a case of me deciding that if I wasn't too sure of the job I was going to just walk out! What a fucking arrogant prick! Was he so out of touch with the real world that he didn't realise that I couldn't just walk out of a job? I would have no money to keep the roof over my head if I did that. Did he not understand that most working people actually need job security, therefore suggesting extending someone's probation period only extends the time in which the employee can be fired with only a week's notice?

Yet again he silenced me with his bullshit. I walked away with my outer-self having somehow agreed to this extension, but my inner-self in utter confusion and turmoil. I met a couple of work friends in a local sandwich shop and told them what had happened. Everyone was in shock. Extending a probation period only ever happens when the boss does not think you are up to scratch in the job. Despite the fact that I had very little to do in my job, what I *had* done, I had done very well so there literally could be no real reason for extending it, other than to simply play games and upset me.

I cried. I felt so very bad about myself. I called the recruitment agency. They, too, were very surprised. They suggested that I go back after lunch and create a list of all the things I had done over the last three months and that I felt I had done well, but that if Rich didn't feel I had, then to ask him for feedback. I did exactly that. I went straight back to the office and began to compile my list. When I was finished I confidently walked over to Rich at his desk and politely asked if I could have five minutes of his time. He looked up from his computer screen and barked 'What is it?' His mood had changed dramatically in the space of a lunch break. I said I would like a word if he had a moment and he said he was busy, so I asked if I could at least have five minutes before the end of the day and before the weekend started. He was incredibly irritated at my very presence, let alone that I should, god forbid, be asking for five whole minutes of his time. He was exasperated and made it known.

'What do you need to talk about?' He snapped at me. I explained that I wanted to discuss the probation period extension.

'Oh, that. Yeah I thought we had decided we're going to extend it for another month'. I said that it was *that* decision that I wasn't very happy about.

You must understand that when I was saying this to Rich, I could not have been more polite or meek. It was so excruciatingly painful to even be in the situation that I was suddenly in. There was literally no way that my demeanour would have been the reason behind his now, very dark mood. What happened next was extraordinary. Rich turned into a churlish, bad-tempered, nasty little man. The look on his face was of pure disgust. He told me he was reading the Bribery Act to which I replied 'Oh'. He replied and said 'Exactly', as if my 'Oh' had indicated that I suddenly realised how far more important him reading that was than my own welfare. His reaction was unbelievable.

He went back to looking at his screen, but I just hovered and must have mewed or made some other similar, desperate sound, without realising. He turned back to talk to me, but this time menacingly. I started to cry and he openly mocked me by saying 'Oh brilliant. That's just great, you crying. How is you crying helping me do my job? I've got a million things to do and I don't have the time for this. I've told you, if you don't like working here you can just leave'.

I replied, exasperated. 'But I like working here for you and Dick' and this angered him further. He childishly replied 'Oh fine, well why don't you go and work for Dick then'.

I was utterly gobsmacked at how our conversation was going. I replied to that by saying 'Oh, don't be like that Rich'. I honestly felt like I was having an argument with a loved one. All barriers had come down and no normality existed. These were the kind of immature discussions you had at home with your family or with a mate on a night out. It was so far removed from what should be taking place in a work environment.

I think I must have given up as I recall walking back to my desk feeling utterly spent. I was broken. Humiliated. He had openly embarrassed me. Made me cry and then dismissed me for doing so. After a few moments, when Rich had presumably calmed down and thought better of how he had just behaved, he reluctantly asked me if there was anyone booked into the meeting room behind us and then asked me to find a copy of my contract, which I duly did. He agreed to have a meeting with me in 'about half an hour'. He could have agreed to this a lot sooner like a proper professional, realising his duty as a manager and he would have saved a lot of hassle.

When we met, it was very uncomfortable indeed. For me anyway. I was weary. My eyes were tired from tears. What followed was very odd indeed. The only way I can describe how it made me feel is by comparing it to the old adverts for a particular orange fizzy drink where a fat orange person would run up to someone in the street and slap them around the face and then run off so quickly that the recipient of the slap would literally not know what had hit them. I came out of the meeting with Rich honestly more baffled than when I went in.

Prior to the meeting I had psyched myself up and prepared all of the things I wanted to say to him about the job – or lack of – and how he had behaved over the last months. I did not manage to say one thing that I actually wanted to, because Rich spent the entire time confusing me with puzzling sentences that had absolutely no substance. Whether he was just incredibly weird or knew exactly what he was doing I don't know, but his mind raced and he went from one random subject to another with no connection or thought.

The only thing I can remember clearly from our conversation is that he said 'I see you leaving at 5.45pm going for drinks with the girls. That's got to stop'. I don't remember what I said to that, if anything. You would imagine that *I* would have had plenty to say about that. You would imagine that anyone would have something to say about that, but Rich had a way of putting it so that you absolutely felt that you could not argue back with it so, like a mute, I think I just nodded. The meeting could not have ended sooner. We had not concluded anything. Nothing had changed. I was still going to have my probation period extended.

Without me fully realising it, I had been manipulated thoroughly by Rich. I had been coerced not only into fully agreeing that I would be compliant with this decision, but had somehow agreed that I would no longer have a social life outside of work with any of my work colleagues. I sat back down at my desk, dazed. I could not wait to leave for the day.

As soon as I left that evening I went straight to the nearby bar and ordered a large glass of wine which I downed as I dialled as many recruitment agencies as I could catch, before they left work for the weekend. I got through to one. They said that essentially, if I was still on probation, I could leave immediately for any job that came up, because with a one week notice period, they probably wouldn't argue the toss if I decided to suddenly leave, given my reasons for doing so. Ironically I began to feel relieved I *hadn't* actually passed my probation. I counted my blessings whilst draining my second glass of wine and with a swimming head, went home to start my weekend.

The following Monday I arrived at work feeling oddly optimistic about what lay in store for me. I knew that leaving was the only option for me and was buoyed by the prospect of joining all the agencies again and seeing what jobs were out there. In a strange way what had happened had made me feel more empowered. Because I knew I was going to walk out as soon as I had secured something else, I felt rebellious and was relishing the prospect of doing exactly what I wanted – chatting to my friends at work, going for drinks with them and finishing at dead on 5.30pm.

When I arrived at my desk, Rich was already sitting at his. He looked at me and winked. I wanted to be sick. He said with a reassuring tone, 'What we spoke about on Friday – you'll get your letter today'. I couldn't have been less enthused.

I replied 'OK'. Why on earth did I need a letter just to tell me what I already knew? Surely putting it in writing that I was being kept on probation was just adding insult to injury and wasting paper at the same time? I was baffled, but above all else, couldn't care less anymore. My morning was filled with contacting recruitment agencies.

The beauty of having a job where you don't actually have much work to do, is that at periods like this, you have all the time in the world to look for a job properly, without the constant irritation of people needing your undivided attention. It was difficult to take calls though, which was the only downside.

Other people in the office were more brazen about it. There was a pretty high turnover of staff at D&D and I would often see people answer their mobile phones at their desk and then walk past Rich talking away and entering a small meeting room for privacy. From the way that they answered the calls you could always tell if it was about a job interview or such. It was so obvious to me and I could never have done this as I would be so paranoid that people knew what I was up to. Instead I used to set my phone to silent and prop it up on my desk so that I could see the screen flashing when a call came in. I would then quickly pick it up and walk away from my desk to the stationery cupboard down the corridor and then answer in a whispered voice.

There was a flurry of activity that morning from all sorts of agencies and by the time 12pm arrived, I could have opened my own stationery suppliers with the amount of envelopes, pens and paperclips I had brought back with me after each sneaky phone call I made. I noticed that our COO was sitting in an office near to my desk when I came back from the stationery cupboard for the last time that morning.

I approached him and said 'I believe I am getting a letter today?' The COO laughed to himself and said 'Well, yes you are, but HR has spelt your name incorrectly so we have to get it re-done. But to be honest I can tell you what it says anyway. It just says that you have passed your probation period'.

You fucking what? I could not believe my ears. My heart sank. After all the chaos, fuss and tears of Friday, Rich had gone and changed his mind anyway. Talk about the ultimate head fuck. I couldn't believe it. I mentioned to the COO about the fact that I had been told it would be extended and he seemed a little frustrated. Not with me, but I am presuming with Rich. He didn't let on much, but what he did say made me understand that Rich had clearly spoken to him about it and that the COO had clearly pointed out that if there was nothing that I had done badly over the course of the last three months, then there was probably no good reason for my probation period to be extended. Or at least that is all I could surmise.

Instead of feeling happy, I felt utterly miserable. I walked back to the stationery cupboard and silently screamed. My buoyant mood was suddenly deflated. I felt very confused and now worried that if I did want to leave, I would have difficulty just walking out. I was trapped. More than that, I was trapped in a job with a man who was the biggest game player and the most insincere person I had ever met; a truly duplicitous man who had just made it clear that I was not allowed to fraternise with my fellow work colleagues. I also very much doubted that my work load would ever improve. I felt sick to the stomach, for the umpteenth time.

CHAPTER ELEVEN

You might have presumed that I would just continue on my journey to look for another job and with even more gusto than before. Unfortunately the flurry of activity with the employment agencies hadn't produced any solid leads, let alone any interviews and before I knew it, I was back in the saddle, pretending on a daily basis that I actually served a purpose at D&D. Rich actually started to give me a tiny bit more work and I had a bit more involvement with his fashion designer girlfriend. Nothing too taxing of course, just a bit of travel booking and the like. Still, it was enough to lull me into a false sense of security for the next month or so.

Unlike a lot of other companies, D&D had appraisals and salary increases, twice a year. It was now July and I was aware that this was about to happen quite soon, with all the secret meetings and discussions that were now frequently taking place between Rich and Dick.

Outside of work, my oldest and dearest friend Denise, had just given birth to her first child Henry. The birth was a very happy and poignant affair because her marriage had been very much on the rocks for one reason or another, prior to her becoming pregnant. Her whole family had been more than happy to see them overcome their difficulties and a baby was the icing on the cake. Both Denise and her husband were overjoyed and everything seemed well again.

One evening only four days after the birth, I received a telephone call from Denise's mum to say that baby Henry had been rushed to hospital as his breathing had become very laboured and there were some rumours of him possibly having had a fit of some sorts. No one knew the exact details and it was not until the next day that we received further news on his progress and a small bit of insight into what had actually happened. I had gone to work as normal, but had told Mike my colleague, what was going on. Mike had his own kids and was very sympathetic.

At about midday I received a call with an update. It wasn't good news at all. Henry was in intensive care in London, having been transferred from Kent. They still weren't quite sure what they were dealing with, but he couldn't breathe unaided. It was frightening and suddenly made his life seem all the more fragile. Up until then, I had thought it very worrying, but hadn't once thought it wouldn't be something that couldn't be fixed and that Henry would be out of hospital within a day or two.

Rich had picked up on my conversations with Mike and had enquired as to what was going on. I told him and he seemed genuinely concerned. Rich had kids of his own from a previous marriage. I never saw him as a compassionate father though. He had the obligatory photo of them on his desk, but they lived with their mother and her new husband and Rich never spoke of them and never had phone calls with them.

At about 4pm on that day I got an email to say that the hospital had diagnosed Henry with an extremely rare condition that affects only one in every 30,000 births. An enzyme that should be present was missing and it is that enzyme that removes ammonia from the blood stream. Without it, the body becomes poisoned by its own ammonia production. The hardest thing to comprehend was that it had no cure.

It was heart-breaking news. I told Mike. I felt so very sad. I had never even met little Henry, but what did it matter? All I knew was that this little man, this perfect baby who had brought so much joy into so many people's lives over just four days, was now fighting for his life. No one can predict anything in life. You genuinely never think these things will happen to you. No one knew what was going to happen next. There was talk of being able to stabilise his condition and if that happened then there may be some hope. I read about the disorder online. Even if infants do get past this stage, they usually died at aged three or four anyway. It seemed tragically hopeless.

Another two days went by and little Henry clung on, giving us all hope. Denise's family are a large, close-knit, loving one, who all rallied at the hospital. I felt helpless as I had to be at work. I was so upset, but trying to be strong. On the Saturday, I went to the hospital as they didn't think Henry would survive for much longer and the parents wanted his aunties, uncles and godparents to meet him. Instead of keeping Henry alive with machines, Denise wanted the chance to hold him in a bed and let him go naturally.

On Sunday, I got word that little Henry had died alongside his mum and dad in the early hours. I sobbed and sobbed for the loss of such a little life. For all of the things that he would never see or hear or experience. The afternoon that I went back to the hospital, I was invited to go and see Henry again. He looked so beautiful and peaceful, wrapped in a little muslin cloth and a tiny woollen hat on his head. I kissed his forehead. Words cannot describe how sad it felt to look at such tiny baby, knowing that he would never again move or breathe or talk. When I left, I sobbed for Denise who still had the full tummy where he had grown for nine months. It just seemed so cruel.

The rest of that Sunday was understandably, very sombre. I didn't sleep much that night, but nevertheless had to be up early on the Monday morning, because for the first time I had been asked to cover Mike's job while he was on holiday. Something I was not looking forward to.

*

The timing could not have been worse. The last thing I had wanted to do was have to be in the office at 7am. Mike's job was a very dull job indeed, made more meaningless after what had just happened on the Sunday. The reason for such an early start is that all mentions of our clients in adverts or similar had to be collated and put into a press round-up and sent to a rather hefty distribution list no later than 9am and as I had never done this before, I needed to give myself a head start.

I pressed send on the first email just before 9am and Rich appeared in the office with his usual cup of coffee. He feigned his usual interest in me and asked how my weekend had been. I explained that little Henry had died. He gave his condolences. He decided to wax lyrical about it being for the best rather than waiting to see if poor Henry might have survived another few years and the sorrow being even worse when you would have to say goodbye at that point instead.

I seriously had no interest in listening to any words of wisdom from a man like him. I too, feigned interest in what he had to say and then got back to my usual daily tasks of doing nothing. The problem with starting so early in the morning and on so little sleep meant that by 11am I felt like I had already done a whole day's work and I was ready for bed. I couldn't wait for lunch time so I could at least find a quiet spot in the only bit of park nearby and try and catch up on some sleep.

The afternoon dragged too. I was emotionally and physically drained. Rich had been intensely monitoring press all day for a release from another of our larger clients – a jewellery company based in Paris. I had literally had nothing to do all day. Dick was not in the office and with Mike being away and me feeling as I did based on the weekend's events; I found it very hard to keep going.

At just before 5pm I knew I couldn't deal with it any longer. The other team assistants in the office had a system whereby if they had come in early to work, then they would be allowed to leave earlier that same day. I had been in the office since 7am so figured that if I asked Rich if I could leave on time, i.e. at 5.30pm, then he might just offer to let me go now instead, at 5pm. I thought that once he realised what time I had been in that morning, plus the fact that he knew what I had been through on the Sunday, he would be sensitive to the situation.

I approached his desk and said 'Would you mind if I left on time today please?' He looked incredibly puzzled for a moment and asked 'Why?' 'Because I was in at 7am doing the work for Mike as he isn't here' I answered. 'But why do you need to leave?' Rich replied. 'Well, because I'm tired' I said. I was flummoxed as to why I even had to answer. It was the wrong thing to say though. Wrong, wrong, wrong. I never in a million years thought that Rich would query me asking such a small favour at such a time. I should have known better. 'You're tired?' I'm tired every day! I'm sorry, but no. I need you here. I've got this really important release coming out and I need you here. Sorry.'

I was dumbfounded. It's not like I was even asking to leave early! I was asking if I could leave at the time my contract stated I was allowed to leave! I asked 'Do you have any work for me to do?' The familiar, irritated face appeared. 'Well, no, I don't, but that's not the point! I might need you for something so I need you to stay.' I should have walked out of that office there and then. Instead, I stayed. I had no fight left in me. I walked silently back to my desk. The urge to cry was unbearable. My tears reached my eyes. I dug my nails into the palms of my hands to create a distraction. My tears retreated. I was being held hostage. Once 5.30pm hit I sat wondering when exactly my captor would release me.

At 6.45pm, just 15 minutes shy of me having done a 12 hour day, Rich called across to me. 'I'm done thanks. You can go'. I was utterly deflated. That night I sobbed silently on my train home whilst looking out of the window so that no one could see me.

The next day I decided to finally speak out about Rich. Being held for no reason was the straw that had broken this camel's back. I had a couple of meetings with some friends in the stationery cupboard to see what they thought the right thing to do was. The general consensus was that, although our HR department consisted of one French lady who, on the whole looked like a rabbit caught in the headlights whenever you approached her with any question, the only thing I could do was speak to her about Rich's behaviour.

I walked into Francine's office and asked if I could have a word in private, indicating not in her office because she shared it with Ian, our IT guy (this was another balls-up by our company, because who would put the HR department with another department where you could never have confidential discussions of a sensitive nature?!).

Francine, as usual, looked slightly horrified that she had even been approached, but nevertheless, promptly rose from her seat and followed me to one of the boardrooms at the other end of the office, away from prying eyes. I closed the door and we both sat down opposite each other across a large, white Plexiglas table. I began to explain why I wanted to talk to her and without any real warning, the tears started to flow uncontrollably from my eyes. One by one they dropped down my cheeks, taking my mascara with them.

Months of sheer frustration crumbled and dropped to the table in front of me as I explained how Rich had been treating me. I explained about the Dick situation and the email I had received in the first few weeks, the lack of any work, the controlling behaviour, the death of Henry, the lack of compassion and the sheer oddness of Rich. Francine was shocked that it had got to this stage without me having said anything. She said she was very sorry that this had been happening to me. I guess I wanted to know if Rich had any right to hold me in the office after my contracted hours had finished, with no actual work to do. She told me it was completely inappropriate and not right for him to have done this.

Aside from this she was pretty useless though. She told me that if it were a complaint about anyone else in the company she would speak to them, but because it was about Rich, she couldn't possibly speak to him. To be honest I wasn't that surprised at this. I kind of knew that Francine had only been employed as a box-ticking exercise a couple of years back. Because D&D were now owned by a larger company, they had felt a need to be more corporate for protocol's sake. Neither Rich nor Dick took Francine seriously. HR was there to deal with the plebs in the office, but the owners could do what they wanted.

The only choice I had was to speak to the COO who had known both Rich and Dick for years. Francine offered to speak to him for me, but tried her very best to persuade me that it would be best coming directly from me. I agreed and left the boardroom feeling like my meeting had been an entire waste of time. There was really no time like the present so I went to the ladies to fix my face before popping into the office where the COO, Harry Dakin sat.

Harry was an odd chap. I'd not really taken to him in my time at D&D. He was rarely friendly. I recall my first encounter with him was when I had popped into his office to ask him about my contracted hours, which had been typed up on my letter of engagement as being 8.30am until 6pm. I had been assured by one of the secretaries that you could only be on one shift of work or another, you either started at 8.30am or 9am and finished accordingly at either 5.30pm or 6pm. Harry had reluctantly agreed that this was correct and agreed to have my contract amended, but ensured that before I left his office, I was fully aware that, had he had his way, 'you would all work 7 until 7!'. What a pleasant thing to hear on my first day in the job, I had thought at the time.

I approached Harry when I saw he was alone (he shared an office with the CFO and an accounts lady). He didn't hesitate in welcoming me into the office. We decided that the best place to talk would be away from the view of both Rich and Dick, so we went to the breakout area which was rarely used in the morning. I found it difficult to know where to begin telling Harry what had been happening. I became teary again, but nothing like the flood of emotion that had ensued when I had been talking to Francine.

Surprisingly, Harry was very sympathetic. Reading between the lines, he was not unused to people being upset at Rich's behaviour. He agreed completely that Rich having held me back when I had no work to do, especially after such an emotionally draining time, was not on. He assured me that he would have a word, but would put it in such a way so as not to seem like I was 'moaning for the sake of it', because knowing Rich as he did, he would surely see it that way.

I was worried that after this had happened, it would be obvious as I feared tension would be in the air. I was frightened that Rich would be angry and start to be even meaner to me. It's a horrible thing to be that scared of standing up for yourself. This is how bullies work though. They make you frightened to speak out. I was on edge for the rest of that day plus the next, wondering when I would sense a shift in mood. Nothing happened. Nothing that I was expecting, anyway.

Incredibly, Rich seemed to get nicer in the days that followed. It was a relief to be honest. After what had recently happened, I was happy not to be doing much. Doing nothing too taxing satisfied me temporarily. That and swimming at the gym downstairs. I kept as low a profile as I could over the next few weeks.

CHAPTER TWELVE

I had a catch-up with Rich at the end of July. Since I had spoken to Harry two weeks prior, Rich had been altogether more pleasant, but I still hadn't been given much more work to do. Therefore to be told by him in our review that I was now heading on the 'right trajectory' seemed incredibly stupid. I hadn't been doing anything more or less than I had been months earlier.

I figured that I would use the opportunity to ask about a pay rise. What did I have to lose? He could only say no – which he did. Not only did he say no, he also took great pleasure in informing me that he knew exactly what 'secretaries' were worth and the information I gleaned from our meeting was that as long as I stayed at D&D, I would never earn much more than I was on now. The only thing that had ever kept me going throughout all of the pain, was that I knew I would get a salary increase and a bonus at some point. To be told pretty much that I would never get this was a big, fat kick in the teeth. I knew then, that it was definitely time to move on.

Now however, I was more determined than ever to move up substantially in salary and I would not stop until I had moved into the executive pay bracket. This would mean moving up by at least ten grand. Not an easy thing to do, I soon discovered.

A PA in London can be paid anything between the £20,000 to £40,000 bracket as a basic starting salary. Once you move up to £45,000 and beyond, it is generally thought of as 'danger money'. You would expect to be on call 24/7, available at the drop of a hat to every whim of your boss, whether it impedes on your free time or not. If you are lucky enough not to have a boss who expects this, then he will get his pound of flesh in some other way – either the job itself will be a horrendously hectic and difficult one or you will get an absolute arsehole of a boss who pays through the nose for you because he just wants a punch bag. You will always find PAs who earn in excess of £80,000 also, but they are usually PAs who started out on a lower level and have stayed loyal to their boss and vice versa and have been rewarded as such over the years.

What I found when I started to look at the higher paid PA jobs is that the jobs which are pleasant and pay well, are usually filled by long-standing candidates and the only time they ever become available are either when the PA retires or decides to make a dramatic change like leaving the country – two things that rarely happen. The PA jobs that come on to the market that appear too good to be true usually are just that. Even if the hours seem good and the pay is what you are looking for, then the catch is usually that the boss is a wanker and his reputation will be well known, but the recruitment agencies don't always tell you this because they want to get a candidate into the job and make their commission.

Signs to look out for re the boss when being sold a job are:

'He is a character' = He is really bad tempered.

'He can be slightly difficult' = He is really unreasonable with a complete lack of patience.

'He can be challenging' = He's a wanker.

'He's a real go-getter' = He's a wanker.

'He's got a larger than life personality' = He's a wanker.

Now, there are different degrees of difficulty and not all bosses fit into the same mould.

There are bosses who are downright rude and make it really difficult for you to talk to them, because you are considered beneath them. That's one kind of difficulty because you can't always do your job properly due to the lack of communication, so that's a drag. Not altogether unworkable though, so I suppose you can deal with it as long as the hours are OK and the salary is acceptable.

Then you get the bosses who are totally unpredictable and never consistent in their personality. The bosses who arrive at the office already in a foul temper and leave you thinking it must be something you have done, or rather not done. You spend your entire morning freaking out thinking that your boss hates you and that you are about to get the sack and the reason they are giving you the silent treatment is because they don't quite know when to broach the subject.

I once had a boss who every so often would go into a mood for about three days and every time I was convinced it was because he had discovered that I had stolen some stationery from a former employee once upon a time. Either that or he had finally found out that I was awful at filing and had been keeping three months' worth of documents in my bottom drawer. Every time though it would always turn out to be something totally un-work related.

There are also the bosses who like to play games with you, like Rich. Controlling games to see how far they can test you until you bite back. How the hell these supposedly busy people have even got the time, let alone the mental energy to play these games is beyond me. Rich must have sat at his desk plotting ways of how to drive me mad or torture me. Otherwise he would have surely been so engrossed in his important work that he simply wouldn't have the time to think about me going out for drinks after work with the girls, let alone that I actually had friends in the office.

Some people do genuinely need a PA though, because they simply have too much going on in their lives and can't cope without one. Then there are others who are just considered important to the company and therefore their ego deserves an assistant, even if they rarely have the workload to justify one.

I had to seriously start thinking about all of the above whilst considering what my next move was going to be. I was more determined than ever to move, as the only other friend I had near to me in the office had just been offered another job so would be moving within a month. She had been the only thing to save my sanity over the last few weeks.

We had gotten into a habit of pretending to do training on various procedures in one of the meeting rooms, when in fact all we had been doing was taking wine usually reserved for office functions, from the main catering kitchen, pouring it into coffee cups and getting sloshed whilst trying to keep our giggling down to a low volume. It had seriously kept me sane, being able to vent and let off steam during the difficult times with Rich. Now she would be going though, so I had to work quickly to find something for myself.

I signed up to as many extra recruitment agencies as I could find. The biggest pain about using agencies is that you need to take time out to go and interview with each one before you can even be considered for an actual interview with an employer. So in essence you are taking double the time out from work which sometimes is just not viable. Some people use dental appointments or doctors' visits as excuses. Some people simply book time off from work to attend interviews, but this isn't always possible if you have no idea when an interview is going to crop up. Others call in sick. I had done this once before, but my interview ended up being scarily close to where my actual job was and the utter paranoia of bumping into a colleague or my boss on the underground, just wasn't worth the strain, so I never did that again.

I never liked giving the impression that I was looking for

a job. I was a stealth operator. I used to keep it all completely secret and I made sure that any interviews were conducted at my convenience i.e. way before I started work, after I had finished, or at lunch times. I got a lot of lunch time appointments. They didn't always go smoothly. Sometimes the journey would be 20 minutes to get somewhere and 20 minutes back which barely left any time for a proper interview if I stuck to the lunch 'hour'.

I once was so late coming back to the office I was wracking my brains for good freak act-of-god reasons why I should not go back in at all; rather that than actually have to squirm my way through explaining my lateness – I contemplated travelling all the way home after one afternoon interview (as I had so far taken two hours and wasn't even close to being back in the office) and emailing Rich to tell him I had suddenly fainted and thought it best to go home. Rich used to go to the gym every day at just before 1pm. He was never usually back at his desk before 2.30/2.40pm, so I always knew I had a window to get back in time.

On this particular occasion I knew the tube would take forever so I had hailed a black cab thinking it would be quicker, only to run into horrendous traffic. The cab took so long I was in danger of not even having enough money left to complete the journey, as his meter had just kept ticking. I had asked the cabbie to take me as far as he could and then I had to get out and jump on the tube after all. By the time I got back to the office (because I had thought better of my pretending I had fainted plan), I was drenched in sweat. It was by now 2.55pm and I was sure Rich would be sat at his desk cursing me and I would have to confess all.

My only plan was to enter via the back way. Our lifts used to open on the 9th floor and you could either go to the right if you were a member of staff, or go to the left if you were a visitor. From reception the offices went in a complete circle so I could reach my desk (which was effectively at the back of the circle) from a different entry point rather than walk the long way down the office and risk doing the walk of shame. On the way to my desk I hung my jacket in a cupboard and collected a mound of paper from stationery so that if Rich was sitting at his desk, I could at least pretend I had been there all along, but in the stationery cupboard doing hard work, like, erm, tidying. It was my only hope.

I turned the corner with my wad of paper. Rich's desk was empty. I was so relieved, but utterly exhausted. My hair was still damp from the sweat that had poured like a river from my hot head as I had negotiated the underground, two station changes and a sprint back to the office. I vowed there and then that I would never do a lunch time appointment again.

I started getting a lot of phone calls from agencies about jobs they wanted to put me forward for. The problem was that they were all being offered with a maximum of £40,000 and I was now determined to move up into the big league. I was telling everyone that I wanted to be considered for £50,000 and £60,000 jobs. I was so desperate to get out though, that I was also saying yes to the £40,000 jobs, not thinking they would actually come to anything, but at least physiologically I would feel like I wasn't stagnating. I had a week's holiday booked to Ibiza that I was about to depart on just as the phone started ringing with jobs at £50,000.

I could not believe that it was all happening just at the time that I would not be able to attend interview. Three came in one week, all asking if I could be free to attend interview the week after, at the very time I would be sunning myself in Ibiza. I was so frustrated, but there was nothing I could do. I needed my holiday as much as I needed these interviews. I had to just tell myself that if it was meant to be then it would be.

A couple of weeks prior to going away I attended a bunch of interviews, including one in particular that sticks out because it was just so awkward. I am usually pretty confident in interviews. In this particular interview, I had been told I would be meeting with the head of HR. She turned out to be a woman who looked, dressed and acted like a teenage girl. She was busty and was wearing a lace trimmed vest top with a cardigan over the top, but her massive boobs just kept spilling out and it didn't help that she had really bad posture so kept leaning forward. I was the polar opposite in my neat trouser suit. She had the audacity to look at me as if I was something that had been dragged in from the streets. She had no idea how to take me and had absolutely zero sense of humour.

I tried changing tack and being a bit more serious, but I got nothing from her. There was no warmth, nothing to bounce off. It was a truly depressing interview because I think she took one look at me at the outset and decided she didn't like me so I was doomed from the beginning, no matter what I said or did. I tried being myself. I tried being something I wasn't. I was so desperate to get to the next round where I would be interviewed by the actual boss, and get closer to a £50k job, but could not get past this fat, lump of a moody bitch for love nor money.

Based on the experience, I really didn't hold much hope for my next interview that had been scheduled. I got a call about one of the £40k jobs asking me to attend interview. They wanted to see me just before I flew and as it was the only interview I could actually attend, I went along just for the sake of interview practice. I was as casual, calm and breezy as ever and it worked in my favour, *unfortunately*. I was interviewed by two of the loveliest ladies I think I have ever met. They really warmed to me and my sense of humour. It was a thoroughly agreeable meeting. I knew they liked me and I knew they would invite me to a second interview. I left the building and my heart sank. I knew deep down that I wouldn't accept the job if they were offering only £40k.

My stupid, greedy, stubborn-self had really made its mind up on what I was worth and what I now wanted and I blamed this on Rich and what he had persistently told me from the beginning, about what he thought secretaries were worth.

Predictably, the very next day I had a phone call in the morning from the recruitment agency to tell me that the ladies had indeed loved me and wanted me to go back and interview with the boss. I felt a mixture of feelings. I felt flattered and had that initial buzz of knowing that someone likes you, but a sinking feeling because I knew I would not be happy if I accepted a job on that salary and I also felt a huge surge of guilt, because I knew now that I was going to disappoint these people and I hated disappointing people.

The agency arranged a second interview for me on the week I would get back from Ibiza. I was hoping against hope that I would miraculously have interviewed for one of the £50k jobs and been offered it by the time this came around, so I would have a valid reason for turning it down. Deep down I knew this was an outlandish prospect though and that I would have to face the music and make a tough decision on my return.

CHAPTER THIRTEEN

Ibiza came and went and was what I had needed, although I had been frustrated in part because I had only sporadic access to email. I had been desperate to hear about any of the other jobs and was convinced that me being on holiday would scupper my chances of securing an interview. When I had been able to log on to my emails I had discovered an email from an agency asking if I could interview for one of the £50k jobs. It sounded perfect.

It was being PA to the owner of a property company. I felt certain that I was right for the job. The agency had asked if I could interview during the week I had been in Ibiza. Explaining that I was on holiday, but also expressing my interest in the role, I asked if they would see me as soon as I returned from my holiday. I became fixated on the job throughout the week. At the end of the week I finally had a reply to say that the job had been put on hold, which made me miserable and convinced it was because I was on holiday and unable to interview.

On my return to the UK I was able to check my emails properly, but I had heard from no other agency about any of the other £50k jobs and before I knew it, the day of the second interview for the job that I *didn't* want, had come around. I met with the guy who was head of advertising and marketing.

He was actually great. We got on well. I knew he liked me. I knew I would be offered the job and I felt petrified on leaving the building, that I would have to make a decision one way or another and very soon. I had become so obsessed with proving Rich wrong and showing him that you *can* get a job as a PA paying more than he would, that I had lost sight of what is actually important, which is to enjoy your job and get on with the boss. My head and heart were saying two different things. It felt like torture already and I hadn't even been offered the job.

The very next morning two things happened. I had been given a task to scan one of the papers for a particular advert for one of our clients. I wouldn't normally have looked at *The Times* newspaper, but as I was carefully scanning each page, I came across a job advert that took up half of one.

My heart started to race because it was for the job as senior PA for the property company, that I had been told was on hold. Seeing it in black and white and advertised in *The Times* made me feel sick. Had they lied to me? Was it still on hold, but this was an old advert? Or had the company just decided that agencies weren't getting the right candidates in and so had turned to advertising themselves? I wanted this job more than anything, but was now convinced that as it had been advertised in such a wide-read newspaper, they would be inundated with applications and I would not stand a chance.

The second thing that happened that morning was that I received a phone call from the agency about the job I had interviewed for the previous day. I was in no hurry to answer the phone. Blasé as it sounds, I knew what the outcome was and I didn't want to hear it. I didn't want to have to make that awkward decision. I left it for most of the morning before walking into the stationery cupboard and calling them back. The job was mine. I knew it. I didn't know what else to say other than ask if there was any way they would increase the salary. The agency sounded surprised, but said they would ask what the final salary was and whether there was any movement on it. I was desperate to leave D&D. I had a job offer on the table.

The agency got back to me very quickly. The offer was £40k plus benefits. I said I would have a think and get back to them. I didn't take long. I wanted to nip the situation in the bud. I sent an email to them. I felt massively guilty, but then got pretty annoyed at the eventual response from the agency woman, because I knew what I wanted and didn't want to be persuaded otherwise:

From: V Knowles Sent: 13:12 To: A*** M******* Subject: MTW

Hi A***,

Having thought deeply about it, I would like to say thank you very much to you and to them for the opportunity, but at this stage in my life I cannot move for that salary, which is a real shame.

I really would like you to pass my gratitude on to them for taking time to see me and in no way did I ever intend to waste their time, or yours, and I genuinely would have loved to have worked with A** and his team, but in my heart I know I cannot take the risk of possibly earning that amount of money for at least another year with no guarantee that my situation would ever change that dramatically. As we are all aware the cost of living has steadily increased, but salaries haven't and I think the only realistic way of me getting to the level I want is by moving to a higher paying job without being in a job hoping it might increase every year. I totally appreciate that the firm is growing and has a great package, but I personally need an increased monthly salary to keep up with my mortgage!

I do hope you understand. If they change their minds about salary I would be very much open to offers.

In the meantime if you do get anything in at a higher level please do keep me in mind.

Thank you very much.

Kindest regards

At 13:31, 'A*** M*******' wrote:

Hi,

They have come back to me asking what your expectations would be. What would it take (reasonably) for you to accept? Would you be keen on a £40k salary with a salary review after your probation? Or, what basic with their benefits?

A

From: V Knowles Sent: 13:39 To: A*** M******* Subject: Re: MTW

Hi A***

In an absolute ideal world I'm looking for 50k, but would meet them half way at 45k if they could do that.
Thanks

At 13:40, 'A*** M*******' wrote:

I will mention this but it was originally a £35k role so I doubt it very much. Would you consider a £42k salary with their benefits?

A

From: V Knowles Sent: 13:49 To: A*** M******* Subject: Re: MTW

If they can do 45k I'd be happy to accept and would forego some benefits for that.

At 14:09, 'A*** M*******' wrote:

There is no way they can go to 45k. You did know this was a 40k role when you met A**. Are you happy to walk away from this great opportunity without accepting anything in-between?

A

That *really* pissed me off. Or was I just pissed off with myself for having played this whole thing so very badly? I suppose yes, I had really messed them and the firm about if you looked at it from one angle. However, it really was none of her business to be telling me what a great opportunity this was. How did she know what a great opportunity this would turn out to be? How did she know that I wouldn't be walking straight from the frying pan into the fire?

All she bloody cared about was her commission and the fact that she would look bad in front of her client. I sent her an email explaining that I had given my final offer and that I didn't really want to have to go through the toing and froing that was now taking place as I found it too stressful. She got the message and backed off. I felt totally sick that I had turned a job down when I was so desperate to leave the one I was in. I might not get another interview or offer for weeks.

I wanted to cry I felt so low. I wondered if I had made a big mistake. I had to just tell myself that foolish as my decision may seem to others, hopefully because I had been brave enough to say no to something, then perhaps the universe might look kindly on my pluck and reward me with some other option. I concluded that as one door closed another one would surely open…

*

That very afternoon and to my delight, it did. Late that afternoon, as I was contemplating the decision I had made that morning and feeling rather deflated about the whole situation, I received an email from the agency about the property job that I had seen advertised in *The Times*. I was stunned. They wanted to see me for an interview as soon as possible! I had felt sure that it was dead in the water. My heart wanted to burst. Maybe this was karma? I had indeed closed one door and only a few hours later, another had opened.

It was for a job paying £50k. I was almost salivating at the thought. My greedy ego kicked in. Just think what I could do with that extra money. I started to obsess over a salary gauge website on an hourly basis, inputting my current salary versus what a salary of 50k would bring me in each month. I would be bringing in an extra £650 a month!

I started fantasising about designer handbags and clothes, better holidays and never having to rely on my overdraft again for the weekly shop. I could hardly contain myself. My initial interview would be with the current PA which I was pleased about. If the PA was still in the job at the time of interview it was a good thing. It meant that there hadn't been a big falling out because the boss was an utter cock. If the PA was still there *and* doing the first round interviews, it was even better, because you knew that the current boss respected and trusted them enough to let them do the interviews, which was also a good sign.

It also allowed you to ask a few questions, PA to PA, to try and get the real truth about what the boss was like. I had started the last two jobs where the old PA had left and had no handover and no real insight into who I was about to start working for. This was infinitely better. I was excited. Very excited.

I was set to have my interview two days later, so it was all very fast moving. I could not risk travelling at a lunch time again, because it was all the way out in Fulham and I was based in the City. After work would be too late and it would mean leaving dead on 5.30pm anyway; something that I could never guarantee, working for Rich.

The only choice I had was to have a morning interview and fake a dental appointment. Luckily I had a tiny amount of decay at the front of my tooth where years previously I had had a small composite put in, which had recently fallen out. Instead of bothering to get it fixed, I had been using some temporary dental filling to fill the hole every now and then.

I knew that Rich would be nosey enough to wonder why I was booking a sudden dental appointment with only two days' notice and it would probably require some serious acting by me, so I figured I'd show him the tiny hole in my tooth and then fill it myself on the morning of my interview so I could show him the results when I walked in the office. This may sound utterly ridiculous, but I knew Rich well enough to know that he would be suspicious.

On the day itself, I made the long journey from my home

in Greenwich to Fulham for my 8.30am interview. It was not going to be an easy, quick journey, but for a £50k salary I wasn't going to complain. I got off the tube at Fulham Broadway and made my way to the location with my printed Google map. The office was tucked away behind residential streets, which felt quite cosy and inviting and altogether less hectic than the City. I reached it at about 8.20am. My journey would take me an hour – not too bad I thought. I was greeted by a lovely smiling receptionist on my arrival and shown to the boardroom upstairs.

These offices were not like other offices. They had been purpose built by the Company so it felt more like a residential home than a corporate hub. I liked that though. There was an extensive collection of artwork on the walls – not just pictures either. There were sculptures and amazing murals on walls. I had been told that the man who I would be PA to, Mr David Wilkes, was an avid collector of art and looking after the purchasing of new art and the moving of existing art, would be something I would deal with as part of my job. I was thrilled.

I waited patiently in the large boardroom. It had gone 8.30am by now. I casually picked up one of the company's portfolios and leafed through the various properties that David owned and had developed. He owned the majority in London, but had some interest in the USA. The company was called Arena Construction. They owned a lot of commercial property which they did up and let out. I didn't know much more about the company so was raring to ask questions.

By 8.50am I still had not been seen by anyone. I felt a little strange sitting there like a lemon. I had drained the glass of water I had been given on arrival. I checked my work Blackberry to ensure no disasters had taken place. Not that I would have expected much to have happened before 9am, but at least it kept me occupied whilst waiting for the PA to show up for my interview. Finally at just before 9am, and not long before I'd have walked out through frustration at such rudeness, Nina, the PA, arrived in the boardroom and warmly greeted me.

Nina was a slim, casually dressed woman in her early forties, with boyish, cropped hair dyed a tint of red. I noticed she was wearing those awful running shoes that are like a second skin that you put your individual toes into. I thought it a little too casual for an interview, but hey, if this is how they rolled, who was I to complain?

She was very pleasant. She had a soft Scottish accent and was very inquisitive and precise in her questioning. I didn't feel anything other than comfortable though. I knew I was doing well with my answers. I really wanted to instil confidence in her that I could do the job because she would decide whether I met David or not. All was going smoothly. The job sounded fascinating and best of all, busy.

I explained that after working at D&D for the past year and a bit, with literally nothing to do, I needed my next job to really engage me and keep me from clock-watching. I was assured that there was a lot of work to be done. I was asked about whether getting to the office a little earlier than my official start time and staying later than the finish time would be a problem. It wouldn't be a regular thing, but Nina needed someone to be flexible on occasion. It was novel knowing that there would actually be an abundance of work for a change. I said it wouldn't be a problem.

Then I realised what the hours were. Core hours were 9am until 6.30pm. They did seem to be quite excessive hours for support staff, especially if I was expected to stay later and start earlier on occasion. I maintained that this would still not be a problem as my inner voice kept repeating the mantra 'Think of the money'. Besides, I was sure that once I had met David and he liked me, then I could easily negotiate these hours.

Just as I was thinking that we were about to wrap up, Nina got on to the subject of David himself. She asked me if I had any experience of dealing with difficult bosses. My heart sank slightly. I said yes and then launched into a huge monologue about how I was well used to difficult bosses, that I understood that it was never personal and that I expected men who were at the top of their game to sometimes behave like this and that it was no skin off my nose.

I had completely lied and all because this felt like a race and I wanted to win. I hated bad bosses, was super-sensitive to any form of bullying or nastiness and in truth never wanted to work for a horrible boss again as long as I lived. The devil was truly on my shoulder that morning, telling me to only think of the salary and never mind that Nina had just uttered the words that made me realise in an instant that David was a wanker.

I changed subject and asked how old David was and she told me he was seventy-five. She explained that David was thoroughly nice on occasion, but that he had his bad days. She maintained that it was never personal though and that it was more like he would come into the office some mornings in a bad mood, but it would be a general thing that affected everyone and was not necessarily aimed at individuals. I relaxed some more and thought if he was seventy-five, he would be a pussycat and I could handle him. Nina seemed impressed and happy with me. She shook my hand and seemed incredibly sincere when she said she would be in touch as soon as possible. I felt confident I had done well and zoomed back to work.

On arrival at the office, I walked the long way down to my desk and saw Rich look up as I arrived. He immediately asked how it had gone. I said 'well' and proudly walked over to show him my temporary front filling. He seemed satisfied that that is what I had done and I felt satisfied with my acting performance as I sat at my desk, ready for another day of doing absolutely nothing.

At lunch time I went out as usual for a sandwich and a sit in the park. I had received no feedback about that morning's interview so decided to chase the agency. I spoke to the girl who had put me forward for the job. She had been waiting for me to call to get *my* feedback before giving me hers. I thought she sounded cagey, so I was now very unsure whether it had gone well at all. I said that I thought it had gone well and that I had felt encouraged by Nina. I maintained that I was more than interested in the job still.

Thankfully my feelings had been reciprocated and apparently Nina 'loved me' and thought I'd be brilliant for the job. They wanted to arrange a second interview where I would meet David and asked if I could do the week after? They wanted to know which day I was free. I said any day as long as it was after work as I couldn't feign a morning appointment again. It was arranged for the following Wednesday at 6.30pm, which meant having to get out of the office on time at 5.30pm.

I realised straight after my phone call though, that it was Rich's fiftieth birthday that day and I had already said I would do something as a surprise for him. Not that I had wanted to, but I clearly felt it my duty as his PA and the fact that it was his fiftieth. I had already earmarked a load of Bollinger that had been left over from a previous work do. Harry, the COO, had agreed to us using it and I had ordered a special cake from *Konditor and Cook*, which is a specialist cake shop in London who make some of the most amazing cakes I have ever tasted.

I figured I would just have to get Rich distracted by gathering a load of people around his desk and making him do a speech. I suspected he would pretend to hate it, but secretly love it. Either way I didn't care, I just needed to get him distracted so I could get out of the office on time.

CHAPTER FOURTEEN

On Monday the following week, I had seriously itchy feet. Having had a relatively good weekend with the prospect of a second interview on the cards, coming into work was a serious let-down. By now, my wine-drinking friend had left and I was very much alone in my corner of the office. I had confided in the office manager, Ali, as I was desperate to let someone know about my new job prospect. It was breaking my self-imposed rule of never telling anyone in the office that you are looking for a job, but I was seriously going to explode with frustration at being stuck in the office with nothing to do, unless I spoke to someone.

Ali and I used to arrange surreptitious meetings in the stationery cupboard where I would tell her the latest. It was the only thing that got me through the day. She hated Rich even more than I did, if that was at all possible. She had worked with him for years and had been the only administrator when D&D had started ten years prior. She thought he was a complete pig. The worst kind of man in the world and she despised him and everything he stood for.

She was certain that he had cheated on his fashion designer girlfriend with a young girl who had worked at D&D a couple of years back. The gossip had been rife throughout the office at the time. Two major things that had convinced people were that after last year's office Christmas party, Rich and the young girl, plus two other employees had taken a cab to their respective homes. Instead of dropping the young girl home first (as would have made total geographic sense), Rich had insisted that the cab go all round the houses in order to drop the other two off first. So that was the first alarm bell.

The second thing had been two employees walking down to the then empty, 9th floor to take a look at what the space was like, in anticipation of D&D moving from the top floor, down. The two employees had walked in to find Rich and his lady in a very compromising position up against a wall. This rumour had spread like wild fire, as you can imagine. I personally had not ever seen a reason to doubt that he was very much in love with Fashion Designer, although I did sometimes think what a convenient relationship for them both.

He clearly loved the trappings that came with being attached to a minor celebrity and she could not have saved her business without his money. I guessed that they were still lustful of each other too. I saw the odd crude email that he sent her every now and then and someone in the office did claim to have once walked by her old ground floor flat in West London and saw Rich 'fucking her from behind across a kitchen table'; the sight of which had made him want to vomit. If you are going to do it on a kitchen table in a room visible to passers-by, you clearly want the attention, is all I could think about that.

That afternoon Rich never came back to his desk. I wondered where he might be as nothing was in his diary to indicate any meetings, but to be honest nothing surprised me where he was concerned as he never told me anything anymore. I could never tell anyone where he was or when he was likely to be back. This frustrated others as much as it did me.

At about 4pm I got a call from Rich on his mobile. He was driving and I was on his speaker phone. He launched into a speech about how he was stuck in traffic and that he was worried he might miss his flight and could I possibly take a look and see what later flights there were. Up until that phone call I had no idea he wouldn't even be back in the office, let alone that he was flying anywhere that evening. There was just no point in him having a PA. He didn't need me. He did everything behind my back and I found out about things, three weeks after they had happened.

I was seriously pissed off. I asked him where he was flying to and he said Nice. I said I would look at all BA flights later than his planned flight which was at about 6pm that evening. Once I had a couple of options I called him back. He sounded as though he was salivating with enthusiasm and told me to go ahead and reserve two more tickets for the later flight, just in case.

I told him I presumed I was booking for him and his girlfriend, and with incredibly unusual speed, he barked back 'No, it's just me and a guy'. Odd response, I thought. I had to press him for more information. 'Can I take his name then, because I can't book unless I have all passengers' names?'

There was a pause. A nano-second of a pause, but still long enough for me to realise that all was not as it should be. 'Erm, actually the traffic seems to be clearing now but, thanks anyway'. He could not have got off the phone any quicker.

My mind was racing! Was he having a clandestine relationship with a man? Why the secrecy and weird sound of his voice? I couldn't wait to tell Ali in the stationery cupboard. Where was he going to? And why was he leaving tonight and – more to the bloody point – did this mean he would not be coming back on the Wednesday for his birthday, in which case I could easily shoot off to my interview? It was all very odd indeed, but suddenly a lot more exciting!

*

On the Wednesday morning I made sure I looked smart enough for my job interview that evening, but not too smart so as to raise any suspicion within the office. I arrived to find Rich sitting at his desk. So, depressingly for me, he was back from France. I wondered what he had been up to. I had done a tiny bit of digging the day before so knew that he could not have been with Fashion Designer, because she had been in another part of the UK.

I reluctantly wished him a Happy Birthday. He was as smarmy as ever and gave me one of his creepy winks. Ugh. This was going to be a long fucking day.

At lunch time I travelled to the cake shop to collect his personalised cake. I had sent a card around the office the week before which had made it back to my desk safely and without too many underhand or scathing comments, which was an achievement in itself. I sent the usual group email out later in the day to all but Rich, asking if they would gather around his desk at about 4.30pm. I figured it was early enough to get the 'party' started and me out of the way by 5.30pm, but not too early in the afternoon to rouse any suspicion.

I had time to get the bottles of bubbly loaded onto the catering trolley from the kitchen, plus glasses, cake and candles and then wheel it around the back way and into a side meeting room, ready to light the candles and wheel it out again. I was paranoid that Rich was going to do his usual disappearing act at just the wrong time and I would be stuck trying to sort the whole bloody thing out when I was meant to be on my way to an interview.

Thankfully he didn't disappear and I started the whole charade of giving a shit about Rich's birthday. He feigned great joy as we all loomed towards him in a cat's chorus of 'Happy Birthday'. He blew the candles out and marvelled at his cake. Everyone joined in the sham. No one cared – they only came for the free champagne and cake. I think the only person who actually genuinely cared for Rich was his wayward, drunkard partner Dick, who had finally managed to get into the office having been missing in Antigua for what had felt like a year.

Dick gave the most rambling speech that went on for an age. It was funny only because of how utterly bizarre it was and the more he went on, the more we all laughed and glanced at each other. This only encouraged Dick to witter on even more as he thought we genuinely found his words comical. When he eventually finished we all gave a rousing round of applause; we were so happy for him to have finally finished talking.

We all took a glass of champagne and I managed to get rid of mine whilst tending to the cutting of the cake. It was just after 5pm, I noticed. I was hoping that most people would carry on chatting and milling about Rich's desk long enough to last until 5.30pm so no one would notice me sprinting out of the door.

Unfortunately, Rich was such an unpopular man that no one really stayed for long and one by one people gravitated towards the communal kitchen to talk amongst themselves, or back to their desks to actually do some work. I was panicking. I grabbed another bottle of champagne and encouraged the few that remained, to have another glass. Rich approached me, grabbed me by the shoulders and mustered up as much sincerity as he could to say thank you for arranging his birthday treat.

Ugh. I felt really bad. I know I shouldn't have cared, but I suddenly felt incredibly guilty that I was about to bugger off to another job interview, when he was actually genuinely thanking me for something. I pushed the thoughts to one side. It was 5.20pm. I needed to man up and plan my escape.

I managed to pick up my bag and coat from under my desk and shield it from view with my body, as I walked away from Rich towards reception. I hid both bag and coat in the post area. I then went back to my desk and hovered about until 5.28pm. I shut my PC down and casually sauntered the other way up the office looking like I was just going to the loo. I then made my way back to the post area, picked up my coat and bag and legged it to the lifts. It was 5.31pm. I had escaped.

I reached the offices of Arena with a few moments to spare. It would have been bad to arrive late when being interviewed by the boss himself. I needn't have worried though. I was taken up to the boardroom again and still had not been seen by 7pm.

Timekeeping was clearly not a priority for this company.

It was annoying, but what could I do? I wanted the job. Eventually David Wilkes walked into the room. He was a tall, wiry looking chap with grey, wiry hair. He smiled and I noted that his teeth looked like rabbit's teeth. He looked pleasant enough. I thought he was probably a pussycat. It would be fine.

He shook my hand and it felt very stiff and awkward. Nina had told me in the previous interview that he had an issue with his hands and had had surgery performed on them a few times. I can only describe the feeling of shaking his hand was as though rigamortis had set in. We sat at the large, round table.

He had an awkwardness about him. He spoke rather slowly

and sometimes tripped over his words. I had been warned that he was rather un-PC and this became apparent when after he had gone through the usual rigmarole of my background, job history and education, he decided to ask how old I was and whether I was thinking about having children at some point.

I was more than happy to answer and put his mind at rest that if given the job, I would be in it for the long term (particularly if my £50k salary was going to increase each year, I mused). The only concern he had was the travelling and he made out that he was more worried for me in terms of what a gruesomely long journey I would have, especially in the winter. I garnered that he didn't take the tube.

I thought he was very sweet to be so concerned about my wellbeing (little realising that at the time that he was really just concerned that as it was such a long journey, there would be a greater chance of some part of it going wrong and me not being in work on time). Our interview ended with him saying he would have a serious think about the travel situation. I was worried that this would be the only thing standing between me and £50k. I tried my best to reassure him that it would not be a problem. We shook hands again and he showed me the office I would be working in, if offered the job. A sure sign that he really liked me, I thought.

By the time I got to the platform at Fulham Broadway, it was nearly 8pm. It was quite depressing as I would only now get home at about 9pm. It really was a long way to travel, but I brushed the negative thoughts to one side and remembered my mantra of thinking about the money.

CHAPTER FIFTEEN

The next day I got into work to find Rich in one of the most jubilant moods I had ever seen him in. It was disconcerting. Nothing had been mentioned about me disappearing without saying goodnight. I felt good and sat my mobile phone next to me on my desk, waiting for the phone call from the agency.

Mid-morning, I was in the communal kitchen with a colleague. We were making small talk about Rich's birthday and how he and Fashion Designer were due to fly out to the south of France that afternoon because they were going to celebrate his birthday on his yacht.

'Yes they are flying out on Valerian's private jet as a treat aren't they?' My colleague asked me.

Valerian was an uber-rich client of ours who we were

convinced was in love with Rich. It would seem totally plausible that she would do this for him as a birthday gift; however I had seen for myself in black and white that both he and Fashion Designer were booked onto an Easyjet flight that day. I queried with my colleague as to where he had heard that from and he said it was Rich himself who had been 'almost bragging about it'.

What an odious little man Rich was.

I didn't mention the Easyjet thing to my colleague, just in case I had actually got it wrong, but wanted to check anyway, so went back to my desk. I logged on to Rich's Easyjet account to see if for some reason the flights had indeed been booked, but then cancelled due to a last minute offer of a private jet. I had to choose VIEW ALL RECENT TRANSACTIONS as I believe he had booked the flights a while back and they weren't showing as current on the front screen.

As the transactions came up on my screen I could see that he and Fashion Designer still had bookings for that afternoon, so I knew that the private jet story was just a load of rubbish designed to impress others. Just as I was about to log out, something else caught my eye. I saw two separate bookings for two people to Nice.

Usually Rich booked for he and Fashion Designer on one booking so for two separate transactions to be showing would indicate they were booked at separate times. I opened up the booking and couldn't believe what I saw. One flight had been booked to Nice for Rich and one flight departing at the same day and time to Nice had been booked for Michelle Olivier. My mouth nearly fell open.

Michelle Olivier was a nubile young blonde who worked at D&D in the accounts section. She was not exactly beautiful, but she was lithe and sexy and about 20 years younger than Rich. My mind racing and my whole body and mind alive with curiosity, I checked the dates of the flights and worked back on my calendar when they had taken place.

They were recent.

The date matched the day Rich had called me from his car in a panic about missing his flight. There had been no guy travelling with him! It had been Michelle in his car all along. She was the mystery person who had flown with him to Nice for two days of – I presumed – shagging.

I was almost thrilled at my sleuthing. I then realised I actually felt sorry for Fashion Designer. She doted on Rich. I was deep in thought when the strangest thing then happened. Mike suddenly raised his head from his desk opposite and mentioned that he had something on his mind and wondered whether he should tell me about it or keep it a secret.

It was totally out of the blue. I freaked out in my head, suddenly remembering where I was and that anyone could have walked up behind me and work out what I was now thinking. I quickly replied and said he should just tell me.

He wouldn't.

I established that it was about some*one* rather than some*thing*. I asked him to at least give me the initials of who he was talking about because I just had a feeling I knew he was about to talk about Michelle Olivier.

'MO' he said.

'Whoah' I replied. Michelle Olivier. I had to tell him what I had discovered immediately. Mike's story tallied exactly with mine. What he had been keeping to himself was that on the morning of the flights and when Rich had called me from his car in a panic, Mike had gone to our shared printer to collect a document he had printed, only to find a boarding card for Michelle Olivier. He had thought it odd, as she was based nowhere near our department.

As he had picked it up, Rich had snatched it out of his hands saying it was his. My mind went into overdrive. This was the single most thrilling thing that had happened in the entire time of being at D&D.

Were the rumours true about Rich? Was he just a serial playboy who had indeed had an affair with the young girl two years ago and who was now having a fling with someone twenty years his junior? Why should I have been surprised?

Apparently he left his pregnant wife to be with Fashion Designer so why would he now be faithful? Leopards rarely changed their spots. Mike and I had to pause and recompose ourselves when Rich suddenly appeared back at his desk. I quickly took a screen grab of the web page showing the flights for Michelle and Rich and shut the website down.

Rich asked me to book him a cab for as soon as possible. All cabs always arrived at the front of our office building. After a couple of minutes Rich asked me what the street was called at the back of our office building. I had no idea, so I searched on the internet for it and told him. He said *that* was where he wanted the cab to pick him up from.

I called and booked for him. He was off to Victoria, where I presumed he would be getting the express train to the airport for his flight. The cab arrived within ten minutes and I got the usual phone call from reception to say it had arrived.

There was a fire door just behind where Mike sat, that hid a service lift that went straight down to the underground car park. Rich would often appear from this door or disappear behind it as opposed to going via the normal route. As soon as the cab arrived he went through this door and said a quick bye to both Mike and I. I thought nothing of it.

As soon as he had gone Mike and I got back to our gossip about Michelle Olivier. Michelle sat at the opposite end of the building in her own office that I could see in the distance from where I sat. I looked, but could not see her. All of a sudden my brain caught up with my racing mind. Something told me to walk to that end of the office.

As I approached her office I was gobsmacked.

It was the middle of the afternoon and Michelle already had her coat on and was pulling up the handle on her compact wheelie suitcase. She had her handbag over one shoulder and a huge smirk on her face. She was going to France with Rich again. She had to be. It all made sense in an instant.

Thankfully she didn't see me. I raced over to Ali's desk to tell her to come out to reception as soon as possible to witness Michelle leaving in the middle of the afternoon. We both raced out and from reception we saw Michelle walk her suitcase to the lift with a spring in her step. Ali and I sauntered out into the lift area just as two more people did. Michelle was suddenly surrounded.

Ali asked her outright if she was 'going anywhere nice?' Michelle flushed. She clearly had not been expecting an ambush and did not know what to say.

Unfortunately for us, one of the other people who had appeared at the lifts at the same time, asked her a more serious work-related question, which she swiftly answered whilst totally deflecting the question about where she was going. The lift arrived. Damn it!

Michelle went inside and the doors closed. I was seething and I wasn't sure why. I walked back to my desk, head full of theories. The cab I had booked to collect Rich from the back of the office must have been for Michelle and Rich had left through the fire exit door because he was driving himself to the station. There is no way he would have taken that exit for any other reason, because it led to the underground car park where he parked his car, not to street level where you collected cabs from.

They *were* off to France together and obviously it was a secret because otherwise he could have given her a lift in his car or he could have taken the cab with her, if it was all innocent. I still second-guessed myself though.

Were they *actually* having an affair or was it something else? Was I being totally naïve in thinking that it could be anything *other* than an affair?

I told Ali everything I knew in the stationery cupboard. As office manager, she was forwarded copies of all employees' phone records – including Michelle's and Rich's. Ali said she would send me a copy of the phone records. I first got a list of dates and numbers dialled on Rich's Blackberry. Ali sent it to me in a spreadsheet, ensuring that it was sent from her private email address to my own private account.

I cross-checked dates when I knew he had been travelling or when I knew Fashion Designer had been out of town against the phone call list. I was particularly interested in the date when Rich had called me in a panic about possibly missing his flight. I saw that he had called me from his Blackberry that afternoon.

The next number that he had called was a number that I recognised. I looked it up. It was the concierge service that you have access to when you hold a particularly exclusive credit card. I worked out that as soon as he had been given the info he needed from me, he had called his concierge service immediately to get *them* to book the extra flights, as opposed to having to tell me the name of the other passenger. Very sneaky indeed.

He was such a liar and he was being less and less like the cool persona he had created for himself. He was making mistakes and leaving a trail everywhere. It had to be true. He had to be having an affair with Michelle.

In amongst all the excitement, I had failed to look at my phone once that morning. I noticed I had two missed calls from the agency and one voice message. My heart soared. The message was from the agency. I snuck off to the stationery cupboard and called them back. It was fantastic news. David Wilkes really liked me and I was the front runner.

He was still concerned about the distance I would have to travel though and wanted me to go back for a third and final interview where I would see him again, as well as the company secretary.

For goodness sake! Why would anyone need a third interview – and *more* sometimes? I had met the man I would be working for. Surely after two lengthy interviews they knew what they were looking for? Didn't they realise how difficult it was getting to interviews on the sly when already in a job? I suppose I was just frustrated because I wanted to leave D&D and each time this happened, it dragged the process on for yet another week.

I was set to meet with him for the last time the following Thursday, after work again. In the meantime I would have to just satisfy myself with being a private detective and looking for more evidence of Rich's indiscretions over the next week.

CHAPTER SIXTEEN

Rich didn't come back into the office until the Tuesday of the following week. I had been thoroughly bored on the Monday, but no more than usual. Ali and I had had our usual conferences, but this time we had been able to freely talk at my desk without Rich being there. Dick had been around, but only ever to show his face in the mornings and then he would usually have a client lunch and not show his face in the office until the next day.

I'm not sure if anything had ever been said to him and that was the reason for him not showing his face much in the office recently, but Ali had told me how late one night there had only been her, Dick and one of the junior account managers, Chris, left in the office. As Chris had gone to pack his things up for the night he had seen that Dick was sitting at his desk, freely watching hardcore porn on his computer and making movements that might indicate he had been pleasuring himself at the same time. Chris had told Ali who had then seen it for herself, and reported him to the COO the next day.

Unreal, but true, apparently.

What a dick Dick really was. He had clearly thought that because I had bought him a privacy screen for his PC that it meant he could watch anything and no one but he could see it. Clearly, he not realised that in order for the privacy to kick in someone had to be looking at your screen from an angle, and anyone directly behind you could still easily see what you were looking at. Furthermore, did he think that anyone would *not* be able to tell what he was doing at his desk?! He was such a dirty bastard.

He was another one I had been told was cheating on his wife. I had seen some evidence of this with my own eyes when I had had the misfortune of accidentally seeing his private email inbox one day, when he asked me to sync his iPad for him. I had seen an email from him to some woman in Brazil telling her how sexy she was and how he had 'made love' to another girl, 'many, many times'.

Urgh. I had been really shocked when I had read that. Who the hell would want to shag that overweight, disgusting pig, paid or not? Everyone in the office seemed to know he was doing it though. It was no real surprise to anyone else.

Ali and I had been analysing the phone records between Michelle and Rich and he had been calling Michelle on her personal number way too many times and at very odd hours of the day for it to be classed as innocent. I was dying to tell Fashion Designer. I fantasised about sending clippings of the screen shots showing the flight bookings and the phone records.

I knew deep down though, that I only wanted to do this because I wanted to hurt *him* as he much as he had hurt me. The reality was that it would have hurt her a great deal more and she didn't deserve that. And, in truth, I didn't have much to go on anyway.

Try as I did, I couldn't quite get any sort of undeniable evidence. It was most frustrating, as I just felt like the slimy arsehole was getting away with it, like he got away with everything else. I was desperate to get something solid and send it to him in the post so that he would at least know that someone else knew. Part of me also could also not be arsed with it at all though and was just desperate to get out of that place and forget that I ever knew Rich or Dick.

Thursday came around pretty quickly. I had arranged to get to my third and final interview at 6.30pm again, which meant leaving at 5.30pm. It wouldn't be a problem this time though, as Rich was going to be out of the office at a meeting and even if Dick was about, he was never aware of what was really going on. His mind was usually in the gutter, thinking about booze, prostitutes or porn, I presumed.

In a strange way I probably would have tolerated working at D&D for a while longer, had I only worked for Dick. Even with his debauched ways, he at least gave me work to do more often than Rich and with such a lackadaisical attitude to everything; it meant the pressure was rarely on.

However, I did work for Rich and as that was no longer tolerable; I knew I needed to give my all in the interview that evening in order to win the job and get the fuck out of there.

*

I arrived at Arena Construction and went through the normal procedure. I was shown to the boardroom with a glass of water and I waited for David to appear with the company secretary, Peter Tithe. I didn't wait too long on this particular occasion, thankfully. David appeared a little more serious than he had on my previous encounter with him.

I had a tiny panic thinking perhaps it wasn't as in the bag as I had previously thought. I knew that there was another person in the running with me. The agency had told me as much. Nina, thankfully, had been very open with them about David's thoughts. I also knew that I was the favourite. I just had to get through this, impress Peter Tithe and surely it would be mine.

The interview went well in the end. David relaxed and all three of us had a couple of laughs about various things. They had asked me about what I did in my spare time and I said I enjoyed swimming a lot. They discussed where I could swim near to the office. It was obvious they were thinking I was the right candidate for the job. I was feeling jubilant.

We all shook hands at the end of it and they were the kind of handshakes you receive when you know you are wanted. It all felt very right and meant to be. I went home that evening, one step closer to finally being able to say goodbye to D&D.

*

The next morning whilst sat at my desk, I checked my personal email account and saw an email from both Nina at Arena and from my agency. Nina was asking if I would mind giving my mobile number to her, as David wanted to call me that morning. The agency wanted to know the same. Did he want to offer me the job or let me down gently? He certainly wanted to contact me. Oh dear.

I was now worried again in case it was bad news. Instead of analysing any further, I simply replied to them both affirming that would be okay and providing my mobile number. I wanted to know sooner rather than later, whatever the outcome. I also gave a time frame for him to call me as I would be able to take the call in a proper meeting room, if I knew when he was going to call. I got a reply from Nina first. David was going to call me in the next ten minutes. I was nervous.

I walked past Dick, who was practically asleep at his desk, following yet another boozy evening. He probably wouldn't have noticed if I'd fallen into a well and never came back. I arrived at the small meeting room at the far end of the building. There was only a small porthole window in the door so thankfully no one would see me if I sat at the far end of the room. I must have waited about three minutes before my phone rang. I took a deep breath and answered. It was David.

'Hello there, it's David. David Wilkes'

His voice was slow, steady and a bit crinkly.

'Hello David'

'Yes I wanted to telephone you myself to thank you for coming in to see us again yesterday'

Oh no, oh no, oh no. He is going to let me down isn't he? I thought.

'Oh no problem David, thank you for seeing me'

'Yes, well. I wanted to say that we really did enjoy meeting you and we would like to offer you the job, if you are still interested?'

Get-the-fuck-in.

I had done it. I was ecstatic. I could finally leave D&D. No more endless days of pretending to do work. No more bullshit from Rich. No more drunken phone calls or vile emails from Dick or his rumoured office masturbation. No more walking on eggshells in front of Rich, wondering whether he was going to wink and smile or give me a filthy look for no reason.

And no more worrying that I would never earn anything more than I was! I was now going to be raking in fifty thousand pounds a year! Oh my word. I really had done it. My patience had paid off. It had been the right move turning down the £40k job. Things were finally on the up.

I was so happy I cried tears of joy when I called Ed to let him know the news.

*

I wanted to hand my notice in as soon as possible so that I could get the four weeks out of the way and start at my new place. Rich was away again in the South of France – this time with Fashion Designer, as opposed to Michelle. I could not have waited until after the weekend as it would have meant delaying my notice period start date.

I was also, if the truth be told, petrified of telling Rich I was leaving. It is never nice biting the bullet and breaking the bad news to your boss. It would be even more unpleasant telling an unpredictable arsehole like Rich and I simply did not want to have to do it, so this seemed like the perfect excuse not to have to.

After calling Ed, my mum and the agency, I left the meeting room and marched straight over to Dick. I whispered conspiratorially to him. I explained that I had just been offered another job that I would like to accept. I really had no need to justify my move, but found myself trying to soften the blow by explaining that my salary was going to jump up £12k, so I really couldn't turn the offer down.

Dick wasn't stupid. He must have known how much of a nightmare it was working for someone like Rich, and indeed him. I expounded on how I would have rather waited to tell Rich to his face (yeah, right) than do it this way, but as I needed to hand my notice in that day, it had been my only choice. Dick nodded, indicating that he fully understood. He offered to let Rich know himself. Excellent. I was so relieved. I only had four more weeks in that god awful place.

I emailed Nina to thank her for having championed me. We agreed that I would have a week off before I started at Arena. My handover period was going to be a long one – five whole weeks. I was a little shocked at how long she was suggesting, but as Nina had no job to go to, she was in no hurry to leave and she explained that there was an awful lot that I would need to get my head around before actually taking the reins.

I figured she knew what she was talking about. Nina had been with David for the last six years so probably had a lot of wisdom to impart and a few tricks on how to handle him. I was grateful that I would be having such a thorough handover.

*

The next four weeks at D&D went fairly swiftly. I utilised the gym swimming pool as much as I could, as I knew I wouldn't have the luxury of being able to swim as often after I had left, or at least not in as glamorous a gym. I knew that to keep swimming I would need to use my local, municipal pool which was pretty skanky – to say the least. A small price to pay for keeping fit though at a fraction of the cost of a swanky gym.

My leaving do was set for a Friday night after work. On the Thursday prior, I had impromptu lunch-time drinks with Mike because he would not have been able to make it on the Friday. A handful of others joined throughout the lunch hour. The lunch hour turned into an afternoon, the handful turned into a crowd and I got royally hammered, rendering me completely useless by 6pm.

I don't even remember my journey home.

All I do remember is waking up in my bed, fully clothed and with face make up still on, at 10pm later on that evening. Suffice to say that my official leaving do the next evening was a damp squib. I felt decidedly ropey and was ready to leave by 9pm. I got a card, a big bouquet of flowers and a handbag as bought by some of the girls. As a parting gesture, I booked myself a cab on the company account to take me home.

And that was the end of my time at D&D Associates.

CHAPTER SEVENTEEN

I started my new job at Arena on the 9th July 2012, just as Olympic fever was kicking in. David was away in the USA on my first day and would be for the next five weeks, which is why it had been decided that my handover should last that long. It wouldn't be that bad. Loads of time to get to grips with everything whilst the boss wasn't there meant no pressure. This would be great.

By lunchtime, I wanted to pull my hair out.

I could have been taught everything I needed to know in roughly one week, I decided. Instead, one week's worth of knowledge was dragged out over five, long, protracted weeks. They were so painful; sometimes I think I would have preferred to be back at D&D doing nothing. At least doing nothing at my own desk would have been more pleasurable, because I would have at least had a computer screen to stare at whilst absent-mindedly searching the internet for pictures of cats on bikes.

Instead I had to sit on a hard backed dining chair to the right of Nina, who for four out of the five weeks, was at the controls. All I could do was sit and listen or watch her. I was given no actual task to do for 20 working days. Nina had her own office. This was now effectively my office, but I felt like a stranger for weeks, a fraud, a spare part.

As Nina got on with the day to day job that she was actually meant to be teaching me, it became more apparent that she would not be ready to let go of it any time soon. Nina was lovely, but mildly frustrating quite a lot of the time. I don't think she realised just how frustrating she was. Instead of getting to the nitty-gritty business of doing the job, she took a lot of time explaining very small things that were pointless.

Nina was an admin freak. She was almost obsessive over the way she used a paperclip, insisting that I had to use the particular type that had a slight bend and that if bent the opposite way to the way you would normally use it, it gave a better grip to the documents you were clipping together. I couldn't quite comprehend that she was telling me in all seriousness, how I should use a paper clip.

It was odd, because all I could do was act surprised and fascinated at this revolutionary new way and in return, Nina seemed genuinely proud of herself. I feel awful saying this as Nina seriously was lovely, but I got the impression quite early on that she was a bit obsessive-compulsive about a lot of things. Alarm bells should have been ringing as to what had made her this way, but I simply thought she was probably just like this.

For someone as obsessed over admin details as Nina was, you would probably have expected her office and desk to be immaculate; polished and antiseptically wiped to within an inch of its life. The very opposite was true though. I can recall feeling a bit scared when I had been shown around the offices by David after my second interview. Nina's office, when I took a good look, was reminiscent of a bomb site. She had a load of metal filing cabinets and on top of those were upturned document storage boxes, full of paper. I guessed that Nina must have run out of space in the cabinets and had therefore had to move on to cardboard boxes for storage.

Once I started though, I realised that half of the filing cabinets were actually empty and that Nina chose to work this way. Behind her chair on the floor, were more piles of paper, piles of books and piles of empty document wallets made of both plastic and card. Her printer had a pile of papers and files on top, making it nigh impossible for anything to actually print out. There was only a small space of carpet visibly left on the cramped office floor and that was where Nina chose to throw her rucksack when she came in. I felt claustrophobic most of the time.

I was also at the mercy of Nina's body temperature. She liked to have the air con on full blast as well as having the window open fully. I was freezing for most of my handover. My days generally consisted of sitting on my hard backed chair watching Nina tackle David's email inbox. She systematically printed every single email he sent or received, twice. These emails would go on one pile on her desk. She would then print her own emails out twice and put those in another pile on the desk.

Similarly to the carpeted floor, there was very little desk visible under the mounds of crap that Nina had hoarded. It was truly chaotic. I had absolutely no idea how she could work like this. I was gagging to take over and start binning stuff. There was no way she needed half the stuff she printed out. I didn't really question anything, because of course this was just her way of working and who was I to criticise if it worked for her?

Thing is, it was kind of obvious it didn't work. From what I heard, Nina was usually in the office at 8am every morning, sometimes earlier. She also was rarely out of the office each evening before 7pm and was known for sometimes being there at 10pm and on the weekends too. Instead of being panicked thinking that the workload was too much, I knew everything I needed to know from just observing the way Nina worked.

She was slow. Unbelievably slow. If an email came in for David, she spent absolutely ages reading it and then re-reading it until it had totally sunk in. She didn't need to though. It wasn't her job, neither would it be mine, to have to absorb and fully comprehend everything that David did. She wasted so much time on reading and re-reading complex emails.

Part of the job was to send a faxed list of notes to David wherever he was, on a daily basis. The notes usually consisted of responses to daily notes that David used to email. The notes would literally be a list of things that he wanted to be done in addition to all of the usual tasks done on a daily and weekly basis. Unfortunately, the list of demands rarely slowed down, but Nina was not very speedy when it came to completing tasks. This meant that when she replied back to David with an update of what she had done, more often than not she would have to lie to him on her progress.

It was baffling to watch Nina work. She would start every day with a definite list of things she needed to tackle that day and by the end of the day she would have completed probably five percent of it, if that. She used to be incredulous at where the time had gone and insist that there was just too much to do, but I begged to differ.

Nina just put everything off until the last minute and then would look at the outstanding list and have to add it to the next day's list. This is why she ended up working so late. This is why she had a chaotic office with piles and piles of papers and files and notebooks with lists of things to do. I was desperate to speak out and say that if perhaps you spent less time worrying over whether you had the correct shaped paperclip you might have more time to actually do the things David was asking. I had to bite my lip though and sit, suffering in silence.

David really wasn't requesting anything that required you to have a degree in science. His lists often looked like this:

1. Please chase Christie's to ask if I can have a private view of a particular exhibition.

2. Please book me a dental appointment.

*3. Have I received the package from Amazon that you
ordered?*

4. What is the latest with the recruitment of a surveyor?

I could easily get answers, part-answers or at least progress all
of the above in the space of an hour probably and yet for Nina
it would take over a day to get anywhere with any of these
tasks. It was quite literally agonizing for me to have to sit and
watch the way she worked. I was so bored day after day just
sitting there, watching her.

I only managed to get information out of her about the daily
tasks I would need to do, by asking specific questions. I kept
a note book of info as detailed as I could make it. In between
me asking Nina things, I felt obliged to be quiet because it
was obvious she was deep in thought, reading David's emails,
trying to understand things that, quite frankly, she did not
need to understand.

It was hard work just sitting still in a cramped, freezing
cold office. I tried to look at my phone and go on the internet
every now and then, but then felt as though it looked like I was
not interested in learning anything, but Nina wasn't actually
teaching me anything so it was a very awkward situation.

*

After two weeks of the same thing day in, day out, I was
exhausted. I wondered if I was ever going to be allowed to
actually sit in what would be my chair, or type on what would

be my keyboard. Gradually Nina became a little more relaxed about me doing a few things.

David started to call from the States more regularly and unlike the first two weeks, he started to ask to speak to me from week three. It meant that I was expected to do things for him, so Nina *had* to allow me access to the computer, which was like prising a dummy from a baby's mouth.

Mid-way through week three, I was sat at the computer and Nina was busy attempting to tidy some of her files up. We started to discuss the office in general and what my new colleagues were like. We inevitably got onto David as he would be the person I would work most closely with. Nina started to tell me about a few occasions where he had been quite difficult with her. I wanted to establish what exactly I would be dealing with. Just how difficult could he be? And what things would I need to avoid doing or saying, so as not to enrage or anger him.

I got a lot more insight than I had anticipated.

I asked Nina when the worst time had been with David. She was not shy in coming forward. Before telling me the actual story, she admitted to me that he could be 'a complete cunt'. That was her exact word to describe him. My heart sank lower than ever before as soon as she said this. I suddenly felt sick and panicked inside. What on earth had I let myself in for? Why hadn't Nina said this to me in the beginning? Well, I realised she couldn't have used that *exact* word, but at least she could have indicated just how dreadful he could be. I might just have thought twice about taking the job.

Maybe that was the point though? She needed someone to take the job and telling me anything more than she had, would have put me off? I tried to remain unfazed by the bombshell she had just dropped and encouraged her to tell me the story of how it had come about, so as to ready myself for what was to come.

It wasn't any specific incident, but rather a build-up of things that had happened – or rather, not happened. I could only gather that having witnessed over the last few weeks just how slow Nina actually was, she surely would have been as slow throughout the entire last six years. Quite a few issues had arisen as she had failed to complete things that David had wanted. I gathered he was an incredibly impatient man.

On this particular day he had stormed into her office and launched into a venomous attack, slating everything at once, from the state of her office, to accusing her of being lazy and doing no work at all. Nina had apparently not shown any emotion at the time, but afterwards had gone to see Peter Tithe in tears, having been berated so badly and so loudly.

Part of me felt relieved. Part of me felt worried. I certainly did not want him speaking to me in that way ever, but at the same time believed that I would never let things get on top of me as much as Nina did and therefore surely never rile David in the way that Nina obviously had done. That's what I told myself anyway and yes, I was probably being incredibly naïve. There was no way of knowing yet what David was going to be like with me.

I was also nearly three weeks into the job. How the hell

could I escape now? I almost resented Nina for telling me what she really thought of David. Had she really done it out of kindness as she wanted to warn me? Or was she childishly pissed off that I had picked the job up with ease and was actually getting on with David and felt the need to bring me down a peg or two? I had no way of knowing so just had to push it from my mind.

I felt down that evening, wondering whether my taking the job was already a huge mistake. I had to rationalise that a cunt to one person, might not be to another. Maybe he wasn't that bad after all? Maybe Nina had deserved the dressing down? After all, I had seen first-hand how slow she was and thought how it might drive a boss a bit mental. I knew what these guys were like. They were demanding and when they wanted something, they usually wanted it now.

I had trained myself to be quick. Not to get bogged down with the nitty-gritty of each task, but to make a start on getting each thing at least off the ground. I hated dealing with stroppy banks or snooty art galleries as much as the next PA, but if it was your job to do it on someone else's behalf, and you were getting paid a shit load for it, then you should get on that phone sooner rather than later. Nina used to put these types of things off. She used to say she would 'ditz' a task until next week. I queried what she meant by 'ditz'. She explained that to 'ditz' something meant to put it off until a later date.

Nina 'ditzd' a *lot* of things. Things that to me were not even difficult tasks. One day I asked Nina why she kept copies of emails and notebooks. (Nina had a drawer full of every single shorthand notepad she had ever used from the day she had started, six years previously).

'Always cover your back. That way he can't catch you out' is what she told me. 'He'll always accuse you of being in the wrong. He can sometimes hark back to something that might have been said three years ago, but I know I can always go back through my notes and prove that he did or didn't tell me something'. I felt it was a little obsessive on Nina's part. Was David really as nightmarish as this all sounded?

At the beginning of week four I was fully in the driving seat. Nina had reluctantly allowed me to take the reins, finally. Had it not been for David insisting that she let me do something, I am not sure Nina would ever have let me have a go. I actually worried on some days that Nina would decide that she couldn't let go and change her mind and ask to stay. On the Monday of the fourth week, I arrived in the office at 8.15am. It seemed utterly ridiculous to me to have to get in so early when David wouldn't have even surfaced until it was 1pm UK time. However, Nina was in charge of me so I had to smile sweetly and agree with all her suggestions. All I could think was that as soon as I started and Nina had finally left the company, I would be rocking up to work no earlier than 8.50am.

The reason for the early start was because David was very particular in how he liked things. There were routines in place. The routines changed from week to week and even day to day, depending on where he was living – and that could be any one of a number of places. The possibilities included:

in London in his Grade II listed house just behind the office, in the country at his huge mansion, his holiday home in Martha's Vineyard in the US, his chalet in France or his home in a very remote part of Scotland. My morning routine today would be:

1. Turn on all office lights.
2. Open downstairs cupboard to access post tray to collect post that has been posted from the outside.
3. Turn on shared photocopier.
4. Turn on my PC.
5. Check fax machine for any faxes from David.
6. Check telephone answer machine for any messages.
7. Distribute post to relevant people, ensuring copies are made of important documents that David should see, including all invoices that require payment that are over £5,000.
8. Keep David's post to one side – fax across any important letters to his house in America.

From then on, my routine was to look at all of the new emails that had come in to David's inbox since the last one he had looked at, or that you had sent to him. He didn't use a computer. Never had, never would; although he was regularly encouraged to buy the latest gadgets by his children. So, he had an iPad, a Blackberry and two iPods. I could tell from his emails whether he had looked at an email on his Blackberry or not. It was a complete faff, but if he hadn't looked at one,

I had to open it, see if it was important enough to be faxed across to America and then fax or not. Either way I then had to mark each email I had opened as 'unread' so that David didn't miss the ones I *had* opened.

Getting to grips with knowing which emails were deemed important enough to fax was quite difficult to begin with. I learned in my first week that he was quite tricky when it came to this. If I thought something was important I would print it all off and then fax to him, but if it was too long, he didn't want it because he was fed up getting reams and reams of paper. If you *didn't* send him something because it was too long, he would be straight on the telephone questioning why you hadn't sent it. It was awkward and very draining, trying to learn which way he liked things, especially as this changed on a daily basis. It was like trying to be a mind reader sometimes.

Aside from emails in the morning, I was also expected to monitor throughout the day. Nina informed me that if he saw on his Blackberry that he had been sent something very important and had not been faxed a copy within two minutes of it being emailed, he again would be straight on the telephone asking why you had not sent it. This in particular was something that got Nina incredibly flustered. When I was at the controls of the computer and Nina was making herself useful, filing on the office floor, she was so worried with being away from his email inbox that she had to have her Blackberry next to her so she could hear every time an email came in to David and check it. She was on edge. It was disconcerting.

I was sent a handful of tasks to complete by David that

week. Some simple, some not so. I got a real feel of just how impatient David could be, with one of the tasks he set me. I received a random email from him on the Tuesday morning telling me he had bought a Yole that he needed to be delivered from France to his home in Scotland in time for him being there in one month.

What the hell was a Yole? Where in France was it coming from? Who did I use to arrange the delivery and collection to Scotland?

I went into a small panic. David had given me no information that could be classed as helpful. I now had to step up to the plate. It was the first challenging thing he had asked of me. I initially spoke to Nina about it and she didn't really offer any help at all, which I thought a bit strange. I went about working it out for myself instead.

It was at times like this that Google was my greatest ally. I searched for Yole. A Yole is a boat. He had ordered a boat. Phew – OK, so I knew what I was dealing with.

I then went into David's sent items and saw that he had been liaising with a chap who turned out to be a boat agent. He was British and based in the UK, thankfully. I simply got straight on the telephone to him and explained who I was and asked for as much information as I could on what it was that David had ordered, who from and where it was in the world. The chap I spoke to was perfectly reasonable to begin with, if a little full of himself. He had one of those highly affected accents. He clearly liked the sound of his own voice, but nevertheless gave me the info I needed.

He told me that this particular boat was being made in France, along with a trolley to launch it into the water. Neither was quite finished as yet though and there was no definite date that had been given to David as to when they would be ready. David had got it into his head that both would be ready in time to get the transport arranged to collect from a port in the UK, ready to transport up to Glasgow, before being shipped across to the island where David's house was. I could feel it was not going to be easy.

I couldn't arrange anything for sure while the actual delivery dates had not been guaranteed, but David was having none of it. In the space of four days, I was made to chase the boat agent about eight different times and each time report back to David on progress. When all I reported was that there was no progress, I just got impatient agitation on the end of the phone from David.

I was beginning to see that he really was a bit of a nightmare. In the end I got the whole thing sorted out, but the boat agent wrote an email to David directly, telling him that in all the years he had worked in this field, he had never come across such a rude and impatient customer as David and that he never wanted his custom again. It was my first real insight into what David Wilkes was like and it was only going to get worse.

CHAPTER EIGHTEEN

I reached the fifth week feeling confident that I could now do the job without intervention from Nina. David was due to be back in the office mid-week so my routine would change again. When he was in the UK the routine was to be:

Monday. Check his emails and fax across his diary sheets (these were two weeks' worth of his calendar from Outlook). The diary sheets had to have every appointment that was his underlined – or if it was a personal appointment then it had to be underlined twice with an asterisk beside it. If he was in the office then this happened, but in addition you had to highlight all of his appointments in yellow. I then had to put all of his post into two separate wallets – one for business post and one for personal post.

(Allow me a momentary digression. The post was a very funny thing indeed. Instead of being given that day's post,

David only ever received his post one day late. He had no idea that his post was a day out of date and, to this day, probably still doesn't. The reason behind this was that a long time ago, when Nina had first started working for him, David had complained (as he often did), that he was not getting his post delivered by 9am. In reality he was getting it most days, any time between 12pm and 3pm. He had insisted that Nina speak to Royal Mail to demand that he got it before 9am. There was no chance of this happening and so Nina, along with the entire office, had decided to simply lie to David and tell him Royal Mail had indeed bowed down and agreed to his demands (this made him feel important). In order for the illusion to work, the rule was that when the post arrived at the office, one of the two secretaries had to grab it quickly and hide it under their desks. This post would then be taken to Nina when David was not about, and Nina would then use this post the next morning, separate it into piles and present it to David before 9am, pretending it was *that* day's post. An utter farce I am sure you will agree.)

I also had to include print outs of all emails that had been received since David was last in the office, which could be a mound. These had to be separated out by 'from' and 'subject' and put into plastic wallets, all clearly labelled. After that it was monitoring of the emails throughout the day and getting on with ad-hoc tasks and on-going projects.

Tuesday. Open David's office door. His office was at the very back of the lower part of the building and there was an interior door to the rest of the office and also an exterior door that backed onto the back garden of his house – the one that he lived in from Tuesday evening to Friday, while his wife stayed at home in the country. I had to ensure I had always unlocked his exterior door for him before he would shuffle across from his home to the office. It helped him if I opened it, because of his stiff hands.

I would then have to change the date on his desk calendar, ensure his window was open to air the office and then place his business and personal post folders on his chair. He received a lot of auction catalogues throughout each week. He was very specific in where he liked them to be placed. Any new catalogues had to be put on the left side of his window sill. If he required you to get prices of what the items had sold for after the auction, he would give the catalogues back to you with a yellow sticky note. You would then need to get the prices and enclose them in the catalogue and this had to then be put on the right side of the window sill. It was all incredibly particular and I was never sure how much of this was his doing or what Nina had introduced him to. It certainly all had that meticulous 'Nina touch' to it.

David would only arrive at the office on a Tuesday afternoon at about 4pm and it often felt as though I was in the office version of Annie the musical, where everyone knows that Daddy Warbucks is about to arrive and all of the members of staff are running around trying to get everything spick and span before he does. The atmosphere changed on a Tuesday. No one ever knew what kind of a mood David was going to be in, so eggshells were tiptoed upon, until his arrival.

Wednesday to Friday. The routine would be the same as every other day, except that David would walk across to the office at about 10am each morning. Every Wednesday evening, Mrs Wilkes would drive up to London and she and David would have dinner in the same restaurant at exactly 8.30pm. It never changed. She only ever spent one night in London and then drove back to the country the next day.

Mrs Wilkes was some 20 years younger than David. I got the impression that their marriage was one of complete convenience for both, although probably more so for her. She rarely had to spend time with him in the week, instead having the run of the country home with its acres of land and staff to cater for her every whim. She had a cook, a housekeeper, a gardener and she was on the payroll, receiving a higher salary than the secretaries who actually did some work. Mrs Wilkes was an artist. She spent her money on art items such as heavy card, paper and paints. She lived a very nice life by all accounts. All she had had to do in return for such a life, was produce three children. By all accounts the children were lovely, as was Mrs Wilkes.

At the London home, where David lived for the majority of the week, he had a housekeeper and cook. She was lovely. Elisa came from Mexico. I was expected to go across to David's house regularly. I would be in charge of all workmen who attended, from gas men to delivery men, ensuring that no one ever entered the house with their 'dirty outdoor shoes on' or were left alone in case they pilfered any of the expensive artwork on display.

On the Tuesday afternoon I saw David's car arrive. At the back of my office was a drive way and small car park. At the front of the driveway was a large black electric gate and at the end of the driveway was a red electric gate that opened onto the grounds of his house. David's Ferrari purred towards the red gates and then disappeared behind them. I made a mental check that I had prepared everything that was needed. Back office door opened, date on calendar changed and post ready on his chair, catalogues in the correct place on the window sill. Had I opened the window though?

Gah! I rushed down the corridor to his office and tentatively opened the inner door. I *had* opened his window. Phew. I ran back to my desk and sat down trying to look nonchalant. David arrived in my office about twenty minutes later. He was very warm and smiley. I relaxed. Nina had been hiding in a spare office and didn't appear to speak to him. He didn't stay long, but thanked me for having sorted out his Yole and said what a cheek it had been for the agent to have written him such a snooty note. I had to laugh to myself when he left my office. He hadn't got a clue what people really thought of him.

The rest of the week went smoothly. I got more used to the daily routine and how David worked. I still wasn't fully integrated, as Nina was still there and up until the bitter end, holding grimly on to the work Blackberry which was supposed to be mine. I also, annoyingly, felt that I couldn't really do much with my office until she had left, because I felt it would be a bit rude to start stripping it of every last trace of her and her six years' worth of dedication to David. Instead, I waited until she left.

Nina's last day was that Friday. I bought her a bunch of flowers, a card and some champagne. If I hadn't have done it, I don't know who would have. Only fifteen people worked at Arena. The majority of them were loyal to David and had been there in excess of ten years. I got the impression that they didn't do the regular workplace things like buying cards or cakes on birthdays. I was also told that they had never had a Christmas do, nor did they ever have Christmas décor because David didn't want it. It seemed too ridiculously Scrooge-like to be true, but unfortunately, it was. I was told to hold the leaving 'party' for Nina some time when David was not around which seemed utterly preposterous, but David wouldn't have liked the disruption. Jesus – who the frig was I working for?

We gathered in the small office that Nina had been using for the last few days. Considering she had been there for six years, no one seemed particularly bothered about her departure. I don't think it was anything to do with Nina, just the fact that my new colleagues seemed to be quite jaded. I worried that it was the effect of working for David for so long…

Nina handed her Blackberry over at the end of the day. David said his own goodbye to her and I found out later, he had also presented her with a cheque for a thousand pounds. Was that generous after six years of working for him? I couldn't gauge. It certainly wasn't a personal gift, but then as I was to find out, David really didn't know how to be personal or in tune with other people.

I ended my day sitting in a local pub with a glass of wine, Blackberry finally in hand; feeling quite satisfied that I could handle what was to come. What I had witnessed over the last five weeks had made me question David and whether I could handle him, but I had a feeling that I could and I was ready for the challenge.

*

Over the following weeks, I learned more and more about my daily tasks and David's expectations of me. One of the first things I did was to completely change the office that I had inherited. Thankfully Nina had moved a lot of the extra files that she had strewn across the floors. When I tackled the desk drawers, I discovered no less than 155 pens stashed away, 65 pencils and enough elastic bands to fill two carrier bags. My office finally felt like an office, rather than a jumble sale. David commented on how I had revolutionised the space. He was amazed and used to tell me so. I was doing a good job. It felt great. I was convinced that as long as I did a good job and was speedy and efficient with time, then he wouldn't feel the need to shout.

One particular thing that was coming up in David's personal life was that he was due to have major hip surgery that October and I knew that it was something he was not looking forward to, one iota. He wasn't the type to tell you this over a chatty conversation though; you usually just knew, based on how tetchy he was at any given time. Nina had made sure she had warned me about the procedure over the handover period. David would be required for a couple of pre-op consultations and she had ensured that all of the necessary medical files were up to date before she had left.

David's files were kept in a locked filing cabinet in Peter Tithe's office. I held the key to the cabinet. I knew exactly what he required and was prepared for his consultation. As usual, David had reminded me about the appointment on one of his daily notes and had told me to get all of his notes ready to take with him. As far as I was concerned, I had all of this already, so was very relaxed about it.

On the morning of his appointment I had arrived in the office at about 8.45am. Instead of looking straight at my emails, I had gone and done the usual opening of doors and windows and sorting the post out first. By the time I got to look at his and my emails, the time was 9am. I saw that David had sent me an email at 8.20am. He had asked me to find something else in particular for his appointment that day. I looked through the files that I had ready for him. I couldn't quite find what he was asking for.

I suddenly felt my face go hot. I hurried to the office with the cabinet. I explained to Peter that I had to look for something else. I knew David would be in the office any minute now and I knew he had to leave by 9.30am as I had ordered a taxi for him. I grabbed as many of the files, as I could. I couldn't find it. David had specifically asked for the blood tests from a particular doctor. Trouble was that David had a few different doctors – some for heart and hand issues and another who was his general private GP. Nina had failed to go through the specifics of each doctor during the handover, so it was a bit like searching for a needle in a haystack. David wanted the last recorded blood test results. I found something. Please let this be it, I thought.

Just as I was absorbing the information, David appeared at Peter's open door. I must have jumped slightly. He looked grumpy as hell already; probably worried about his appointment and the impending surgery. He glared at me shuffling through files and pieces of paper.

'Morning David!' I offered.

'Where is the file for me to take?' he asked.

'Well, I'm just looking for the last blood test results that you asked for. The rest of…' David wasn't one for letting you finish your sentences. He was terribly impatient. I suddenly felt very on edge.

'But you've had ages to get this file together!' he snapped.

'Oh no, I've got the file together. I just was making sure I had the specific document you asked for this morning, but I think this may be it.'

David snatched the paper from my hand. He scanned it briefly and seemed satisfied. I was relieved. Just as my heart started to pump at its normal speed, David turned back.

'This isn't it! This is from last year. I had one done at the beginning of this year. Where is it?' David almost spat at me.

My heart started pounding again. He was so very intimidating. All I could say was that I didn't know, but that I would carry on looking for it. As I tried to look for it, David just hovered close by spewing venom in my general direction, which made looking for anything impossible. Why didn't I know where it was? Why hadn't I been shown all of the medical files? What had Nina been showing me over the five weeks of handover? It was relentless. He didn't let me speak. He just spat more and more questions out at me, not waiting for any answers.

It was so unfair and so uncalled for. I literally felt under attack. I looked at Peter more than once for some kind of help, but he just sat there watching it all unfold. I just could not find what David was asking for and the more he flustered me, the less I could concentrate. David was vile. When he had finished attacking me, he walked off down the corridor to my office. I felt awful. I followed him in and before I could hand him the file, he had grabbed it and stormed off. All I can remember thinking was 'Well, that's the honeymoon over'.

I was drained and it was only 9.20am. I was fearful that David wasn't quite finished and that he would be back for round two. I was really upset inside. He had shouted at me unrelentingly and not given me a second to think or give any kind of answers. I had wanted to say 'Hey, you only asked me for this particular document at 8.20am, knowing full well that I wouldn't be physically in the office until just before 9am anyway, so you didn't exactly leave me plenty of time to find something did you?' But of course I hadn't dared. I felt sick.

David walked back into my office, still with a scowl on his face. He was slightly calmer than he had been. I felt I had no choice other than to just smile sweetly and pretend like

I wasn't bothered. He had to leave and his taxi had already arrived to take him. He asked me to contact the doctor's receptionist and request a copy of the blood test. I said I would and would fax a copy over straight away to the hospital where he was having his appointment.

I felt desperate to make it right. I was pissed off with myself on some level for having relied completely on the file that Nina had put together. I didn't understand why if everything had been there prior, it would not be there now. Was David requesting things that he knew weren't there, just as an excuse to have a go at me?

The second David left the office I called the receptionist at the doctors. I explained who I was and who the patient was and what I was looking for. As I was still on the line and within a matter of moments, I was told that the document I had already given to David from the previous year *was* in fact the last tests that he had results for. He had not been tested so far this year. David had been mistaken. The document he had insisted existed did not and never had. I had been through all of that trauma for nothing. I sent David an email immediately, telling him. I knew he would read it in the back of the cab on his Blackberry.

When he got back to the office later on that morning, he appeared in my office looking incredibly sheepish. He tried to put a smile on his face as he made eye contact with me, but I was already wounded. I had been scolded unfairly and quite ferociously and after what I had been through at D&D, I wasn't strong enough for this. He passed me his appointment card from the hospital, along with the file that had been diligently put together and said something along the lines of 'Sorry, it got a bit fraught this morning' – except he couldn't quite commit to the word sorry, so it came out as a half-hearted 'Sor…' and his voice trailed off as he talked about things having been fraught. I got the gist though. I knew this was his way of trying to make things less hideous than they had been that morning.

Unfortunately, the damage had been done. David had crossed the line with me and I knew things would never be the same again. Up until that morning, I had felt comfortable and happy doing the job. I had been happy to work for him, wanting to please him. I now had witnessed first-hand just how unpredictable, unfair and volatile he could be. Any warmth I had felt for him, immediately disappeared and it was only week nine. That lunch time I walked to the local park. I tried to act normally, by eating a sandwich and reading a trashy magazine, but I felt very low inside. I wanted to cry, I felt so sad at what had happened that morning.

It may sound ridiculous to anyone not in the situation, but I had just come out of a job that had made me feel scared to be myself and now I felt as though I would always be on egg shells with another boss. I didn't want to be treated like that. David had spoken to me disgustingly and had not allowed me to even breathe, let alone defend myself. If this was to be a regular occurrence then I simply would not be able to handle it. I called my Mum, desperately wanting to tell her how sad I felt, but my pride would not allow me to.

Instead I told her that David had been a grumpy old sod and made out like he was just a grouchy old man who had been moaning. It made her laugh and in a way had helped me ever so slightly. Truthfully it had been a lot more than that though. Something had changed in his eyes when he had berated me. He had looked vicious. I couldn't admit that to my Mum or myself though. I needed to believe that he was just a silly old man and that all was now OK, if I was to continue in my job. The very thought of having to look for yet another job so soon was simply not an option.

CHAPTER NINETEEN

Before long we were mid-way through September, and I was totally embedded in the company and my job. My commute was already beginning to lose its appeal. I was only finishing at 6.45pm on some evenings and by the time I got home it was nearly 8pm. I only had a couple of hours to myself each night before I had to think about going to bed, otherwise I would have been a zombie the next morning, which would not have worked, as I always had so much to do.

My original suspicions on Nina not really having the volume of work to justify the amount of time she spent in the office were founded. There was a lot to do, but nothing I couldn't get done in my normal working day. I started to do more and more personal work for David as he became more used to me. Things actually started to pick up and aside from

David being his usual grouchy self with everyone in the office, I didn't really get any more foul-tempered rants from him.

What did happen though was that David started to laugh more and more. There were two secretaries in addition to me, both absolutely lovely girls. The more junior of the two was a really sweet girl called Amy. When I had started she had told me how scared she was of David as she had heard such horror stories from other people about what he could be like. When David started to laugh out loud at certain conversations we had, Amy expressed utter shock as she had never heard him laugh before. He usually just presented a brooding presence in the office.

I started to get told things by other colleagues like I was a 'breath of fresh air' and just what the office had needed. Amy was convinced that David liked me, but I didn't really believe it until one day David really shocked me. Completely out of the blue, he appeared one morning and without any prompting he started to compliment me once again on the office and its neatness. He then told me how efficient I was and that he never thought he could have improved on Nina as a secretary, but that he had. He said he felt there was almost never too much work to give me as I was so capable. I was bowled over.

Perhaps things would be OK after all? Indeed they were for the next few weeks. David was getting closer to having his hip operation, but I knew he was worrying about it. He had opted for a local anaesthetic which I found to be rather gruesome, but each to their own. He had enlisted my help getting a good selection of music on his iPod to listen to whilst the op took place. I also bought him some expensive noise-reducing headphones so that he wouldn't hear any of the procedure. David was nervous, but grateful for what I was doing for him.

I felt we had finally started to have a good connection and that he trusted me. When he went in for his operation, I was genuinely concerned for him. When I found out that it had been a success I went out and bought him a get well card and got it signed by everyone in the office. I passed it on to Mrs Wilkes, who popped into the office soon after the op had been done. She was very pleased I had thought about the card for him. I don't think David had many friends. He was a cantankerous old git if truth be told. His reputation preceded him and as I got more settled into the job, people that I spoke to on a regular basis felt more at ease and let slip more and more stories about him.

One person in particular, who I liked, was Adrian the gardener from the country estate. He used to come up to London once a week to tend to the grounds around the office and house. He was such a friendly, lovely and unassuming chap. He loved a chat and used to appear at my office window and give it a little tap in-between mowing the grass. We would natter through the window over a cup of coffee, but if David ever caught him, he was in big trouble.

David was bad enough with members of staff within the office, but he was utterly vile to staff who worked for him on a menial level. Whenever I had had a bad day with David and Adrian was about, he would cheer me up by telling me stories about how he had been treated by him to make me feel better. His stories always trumped mine. Adrian had been shouted at and called a liar for no reason in the past and apparently David had called him 'an old woman' and a 'stupid cunt' once before. I was horrified that someone of his age would use such language, and to say it to a member of staff was an utter disgrace.

I felt really sorry for Adrian because he was the type of person who took it, because he feared he wouldn't get any other job. It was for precisely this reason that Adrian had stayed for as many years as he had (as had so many other members of staff) and because of this, it had given David a false sense of loyalty. He believed that he was a great boss, because hardly anyone ever left, despite being treated like utter dirt. As awful as it sounded and as much as I hated knowing how badly David treated nice people, as long as he was not on my back, that was all that mattered. It was all about survival in the end.

*

David had his operation on a Thursday and was due to leave hospital over the weekend. Mrs Wilkes picked him up and drove him to the country estate on the Sunday. He was due to be there for the next three weeks as he had to recuperate. In preparation I had purchased a host of medical products to help him. I had bought two of everything – one set for the country estate and one set for his London home for when he eventually came back.

On the Monday I had a phone call from him. He was quite calm and pleasant. He was thoroughly relieved that he had come through the op and that it had apparently gone very smoothly. He thanked me profusely for my thoughtful get well card. I felt a proud glow all over.

There is nothing nicer than doing your job as a PA and being recognised and thanked for doing it. I guess it is human nature to like to be liked or patted on the back for doing a good job. PAs are no different, except that as it's your job to keep giving on a regular basis, you end up expecting the thanks or praise more often and when you don't get any or very little; it really starts to hurt you more than it should. However, as I was getting lots, I was pacified into thinking that all was utterly rosy between David and I, which was a big mistake.

The problem with David being away from the office for so many weeks was that he became very exasperated. Despite his age, David was a man on a mission. He was incredibly determined and involved at every level of the business, much to the dismay of his senior staff members. Although he had employed a director of finance and a director of property, he could never, ever just let them get on with their jobs. He was forever on the phone to them, undermining them and insisting that no decision be made independently of him. It made others' jobs almost impossible to do.

Key figures, important documents and major new developments on certain projects were simply kept from him because it would have been more hassle to let him see every single thing. This made the secretaries lives a nightmare. Every now and then, when one of these little lies would get back to David, all hell would break loose and it would always be the secretary who got it in the neck.

If David was left out of the loop on an email conversation that later would be printed out and given to him by mistake, he would know he had never seen a copy of it and would immediately march into the secretary's office and go mental, demanding to know why they had never given him a copy. The secretary would then bow and scrape and apologise, knowing full well that the reason they had kept David out of the loop was because they had been instructed to do so by one of the directors. No matter how many times this happened (and it happened regularly), the secretary would still be asked to keep deceiving David and so they had no choice if they wanted to keep their job. This of course meant that the bollockings would happen on a regular basis, which was very upsetting for them and unpleasant for the rest of the office.

One of the bigger projects taking place at this time was the conversion of a tired old building in north London, into a brand new conference centre. It was complex. I hadn't realised until I started working at Arena just how many people were involved in a project of this scale. There were contractors, builders, project managers and of course, us. Then there was the client, i.e. the conference centre. It became apparent that lots of things were going wrong and different parties were starting to blame others for the mistakes being made, rendering David very jumpy indeed. He was paranoid that some kind of law suit might materialise if he didn't get a handle on the situation and fast. He cut short his recovery time in the country and came up to London after only two weeks. Everyone in the office was absolutely dreading it.

The first time I saw David post-operation was on a Friday, as I was walking back to my office from the kitchen. He had come up on that day, unusually. I panicked as I realised I was not carrying a piece of kitchen roll under my mug of coffee. David insisted that you had to have a piece under every drink, as he was paranoid of you spilling anything on the carpet he'd had commissioned for the office. Amy had failed to do this once and he had hurled abuse at her until she cried. Thankfully David failed to see me and I managed to sneak into my office before he realised.

I sat down at my desk waiting for him to come and visit me. I knew I would be next. I could hear him next door bitching to Peter about something or other. David walked in like an un-oiled robot. He was using a walking stick. He had never looked more like his age. I wanted to feel sorry for him, but the nasty look on his face made it impossible for me to do so. He thrust a document into my hands that had scribbles all over it where he had amended someone else's draft email. It was an email to our project managers on the conference centre project. David was agitated and it was only 9.30am. He was rarely in the office before 10am most days, so something must have been up. There were no pleasantries, no discussion about how he was doing. He was determined to get on with business so that's what we did.

He asked me to type up the email and incorporate his changes. Once done, I was to distribute to various different people within the office for their opinion. I did as he asked and sent to everyone at David's request. This included the director of property, Sam, who had his own PA, Kathy. Sam sighed loudly when David was out of earshot as I passed him the amended document. It was yet another example of too many cooks. The original draft had been, in his opinion, perfectly written and now David had made a complete hash of it. Sam therefore had to amend yet further. At the same time I gave a copy back to David who also made his own further amends. David gave me his amends back to type up, but Sam gave his changes to Kathy to do. This game went on all morning. In all I think I typed up six different versions of the email in total.

Just before lunch, David came into my office, which was across the corridor from Kathy's. He was more agitated than before. I could just sense a chill in the air and I felt scared that something was going to blow up soon. He asked me to give him the latest version of the email. I gave him what was *his* latest version, not realising there was any other. He started to read and dismissed it and insisted that he had seen something else with a different sentence in it. He demanded I give him *that* one. I explained that what he had in his hand *was* what he had last amended. He insisted there was another version. I was on the spot.

I attempted to speak again but was cut off. The roller coaster had started. His face changed and he snapped back at me half way through my sentence. Oh god, oh god, oh god, here we go again, I thought. Once David started, there was no stopping him. It was like he saw red and couldn't hear what I was saying anymore.

What followed was an utterly horrendous verbal attack on me.

I was trying to punctuate his tirade with explanations. I was trying to stop the deluge of rage, but it was impossible. He was like a mad man. I was so utterly embarrassed at being spoken to like this. I had to call Kathy over from her office to try and help me explain what I knew had happened. I realised that because Sam had been amending the same draft and getting Kathy to type it up, it had been passed to David without my knowledge so I had not been able to incorporate both drafts together. David did not want to know. Didn't care. Would not let me speak for one second. He just kept shouting and spitting. When Kathy tried to help me out, she too ended up red in the face.

It was hideous. Truly awful. Probably the worst I had ever been treated by anyone in any job, let alone my personal life, ever before. He topped Rich by a mile. Nothing was fair about the situation. I was being treated like a criminal. The abuse finally stopped as it was obvious that I could do nothing to help the situation and David had no more gas left in the tank. He walked off, slamming my door behind him, which caused three files to tumble to the ground.

He disappeared upstairs to the boardroom. I was shaking and numb from shock. After a few moments I walked into the front office that doubled as reception. Amy had gone pale. She said she felt sick to the stomach because the noise of David going on and on had really upset her. It was crazy. It was like we were all in this abusive relationship that we didn't know how to get out of. I needed the job though. I needed the money to pay my mortgage, yet all I could think was that I never wanted to come back to the office again. I tried to laugh it off and make out that it didn't bother me. I was stronger than this.

I think I felt ashamed and stupid because up until then it had seemed as though David and I got on. To suddenly be treated like this made me feel humiliated and foolish for having been duped into thinking all was well between us. That was the first time that tears appeared. I cried in my office, but felt very ashamed and didn't want David to see. I managed to stem the flow of salt water enough for me to go to the loo without looking like I had cried, before then getting inside and sobbing quietly. I needed to let it out before it consumed me. As always, a cry made me feel better, but I still felt incredibly low.

David hid in the boardroom for the majority of the day, thank God. As soon as I could leave for lunch, I walked to the pub close by. I sat in a single comfy chair looking out onto the Kings Road and nursed a large glass of wine. I called my mum and told her how hideous he had been and explained that I was drinking wine to get over it. The chat and the warmth of the alcohol slowly mixing with my blood soon chilled me out. The morning's incident didn't seem as bad as it had done before the wine had taken effect.

I knew it was artificial though. I knew deep down that none of it was right. The way David spoke to me and others was wrong. The very fact that I reached for the bottle when things went wrong, was totally unhealthy. I even contemplated becoming a functioning alcoholic just to do my job. Even if I only ever had a boozy drink in the morning and then at lunch, it would take the edge off and I would probably be able to take the abuse and the uncertain feeling I got every day from not knowing what mood David would be in. It was just plain ridiculous that I was even thinking like this though.

No job should make anyone feel like they need to drink or take drugs just to get through it. I was in a temporary haze because of the wine, but the reality was I didn't want to have to use alcohol in order to function in a job and once the alcohol had worn off, I knew that I would still have to deal with David and his mood swings. I bought myself a sandwich from the garage next door before heading back to the office. I felt better than I had, at least.

In the afternoon I got on with a few tasks. I found it difficult to muster up any enthusiasm. Unfortunately once I had been treated badly, that was usually it. My desire to do the job, and do it well, waned. I think a lot of bosses make the mistake of thinking that if they come down hard on their staff and shout and crack the whip, they will get more out of them. It really does not work that way though. I'm surprised more people don't realise that if you actually treat staff with respect and take time to listen to them and give them the benefit of the doubt, you get a lot more respect back.

The more your staff respect you, the more they want to please you and keep doing a good job. It really is that simple, but so many people just don't get it.

When David eventually appeared in my office, he was back to his sheepish self. He was a fool. He always did this. He tried a half-hearted smile and attempted some humorous banter with me. I was having none of it. I was drained. I feigned a smile and carried on with my work. I knew this was David's way of trying to make the atmosphere better. At the end of the day I walked over to David's office to give him his evening notes and emails from that day. I knocked at his door. Sometimes he was not in the office as he regularly popped back over to his house for a coffee or to go on his rowing machine. Clearly though, he was not going to be rowing any time soon, given his recent operation.

He answered. I went in. I wouldn't say that he went so far as to apologise, but he certainly made all the right noises. All I knew was that I didn't care anymore. I just wanted to give him his things and go home for the weekend. I appreciated that he was trying to make it better, but he must have known how I was feeling. I don't think my responses left him in any doubt. We said goodnight and I left for the evening, thankful that I would not have to see his offensive face again until Tuesday.

CHAPTER TWENTY

I could not enjoy my weekend at all. I had managed to get some tickets for the Paralympic Games on Saturday. I really wanted to see the Olympic Stadium and say that I had been. It turned out to be a glorious day. Not a cloud in the sky and the sunshine beat down all day. I was in awe of the stadium. The weather was gorgeous and yet in the back of my mind I had a nagging sensation of miserable dread which would not go away.

It affected not only me, but my relationship with Ed. I found it hard to smile, hard to enjoy myself. I ended up going shopping after the Games had finished. I spent money on clothes and accessories I didn't need. I tried to buy things to bolster my happiness, but nothing worked. I went to bed on the Sunday, sedated with red wine. I would have been lying awake otherwise, going over thoughts of David and work. I woke early on the Monday morning feeling dreadful. A knot had developed in the pit of my stomach and by now the alcohol had worn off leaving me with a vague headache.

I wanted to cry immediately on waking. It was only 4am. I didn't get back to sleep until gone 6am. When my alarm went off an hour later, I felt as low as I possibly could have. I knew I had to just get up and force myself to go through the motions. The only thing I could cling on to was the thought of Christmas coming, because I knew I would have two weeks off.

I used to travel the majority of the way to work with Ed. He worked in West Kensington and often when I could not get a train directly through to Fulham Broadway, I had to get off at Earls Court and wait for the correct connection. Earls Court is where Ed alighted anyway. That morning when he went to say goodbye to me as he always did, I felt so alone and scared about being left. I reverted to being a small child being left by its mum before having to go through the big, scary school gates. My bottom lip started to quiver and the silent tears started to form in my eyes. I knew I couldn't cry in such a public place. I didn't want to embarrass Ed.

He hugged me and all I could gulp out in a whisper, were the words 'I don't want to go to work'. He knew it was bad, but I don't think he could comprehend just *how* bad it was. Unless you have been in a situation like this, you will never know just how certain bosses can make you feel. You can be the most gregarious, lively soul with outward armour that says 'tough cookie', but anyone can get to you with the right amount of manipulation or sadistic behaviour.

When you are trapped in a job and it is happening, it is so very hard to gather the strength to say how you feel because you are fearful that if you answer back you will be sacked. The fear of being an outcast then panics you and all you can visualise is the worst case scenario of being homeless with no money. That's why you go back to work and take the abuse, but all the while you are dead inside. I felt I had no choice but to carry on with my job, but it was so tough to have to walk to the office when all the while all I wanted to do was break down in someone's arms and hear them tell me that everything was going to be OK. I knew it wasn't going to happen though. In the meantime, I had to simply get on with it and count the weeks until Christmas.

Call me naïve, but I truly believed that regardless of how bad I was feeling on that Monday morning, at least David would know how badly he had treated me on the Friday prior and so would take it easy. That was usually how it worked. It was depressing to be in the office and the weather had taken a turn for the worse. The grey skies and drizzle against my window pane just added to my very low mood. I tried to just concentrate on work.

The phone must have rung at about 9.30am. I usually left it for the secretaries to answer as inevitably it was not for me. Within seconds my phone was buzzing green. I had a sinking feeling that it was David.

'David's on line one for you' said Amy. She sounded as worried as I now felt. David never called this early unless he had a bee in his bonnet.

I answered and tried to sound as cheery as I could. From his first syllable I knew I was in for a rough time. My entire body tensed as he launched into a petulant moan about the filing in the office and how it wasn't good enough and how he still wasn't receiving every piece of information that he needed. It was 9.30am on a Monday. Had he even had a weekend? Or had he simply been rehearsing this bile since I had left the office on Friday evening, counting the minutes until I returned and he could continue his attack?

He was such a peculiar man. He simply had no grace. No idea how to start a conversation. No 'Good morning' or 'How was your weekend?' Nothing. Just more abuse. As if coming to work on a dreary Monday morning wasn't bad enough without then being told off first thing in the morning. I couldn't take it. I simply wasn't strong enough and nothing in my body or mind could force the tears to stay where they were meant to be. I was too weak from the previous battering, my lack of sleep, the tears at the station and the altogether miserable weekend I had endured. My tears fell onto the phone receiver long before I managed to get any words out.

When David finally finished his rant there was silence. He asked 'Hello, are you there?'

Like a wounded animal I managed only a whimper. I couldn't pretend any longer. I was resigned. 'I can't do this anymore David. I'm sorry'.

My voice was barely a whisper. As soon as the words came out, I felt such a wave of relief. I didn't care if he sacked me.

I just did not care. I knew I needed to be out of these mental chains that were making me so desperately unhappy.

I found a small surge of strength. 'If you don't like the way I work, then please find someone else, because I just can't do this anymore. I'm sorry'. David's response was the most shocking part of the whole phone call. His entire attitude changed. He apologised profusely. He could not have been sorrier. He said he thought I was brilliant at my job. The best secretary he had ever had. He didn't want anyone else to work for him and he hadn't realised I was so upset.

He sounded so genuine *I* started to feel guilty for having put *him* through this! It still needed to be said though. He needed to know that I had limits and that he had pushed me way beyond them. He agreed that he *had* pushed too far on the Friday and that with hindsight he could see that none of the confusion that had occurred had been my fault. Why the hell when he knew he had been so rough on me did he decide to give me another hard time first thing this morning then?! I just didn't understand him. I was so relieved to have said my piece. I was even more relieved that he had been so apologetic.

We ended our phone call. I was slightly stunned. Most people near to my office had heard me crying on the telephone so figured that something was up. The girls made me a coffee and came in to talk to me. They were amazed that David had been so apologetic. It was unheard of. Most people in my position had been sacked on the spot if they dared speak to David and tell him what they thought. Apparently an old PA of his had been so fed up with the way he spoke to her, that the only way she had felt able to convey her feelings, was by putting them in a letter. David had taken her letter as her resignation and told her not to come back to the office. She had been working for him for over five years when this happened. He really was a piece of work. Maybe I was different? Maybe I would be a force of good for the office. Perhaps leopards could change their spots?

At about 11am, David called again. This time he could not have been gentler with me. He had only telephoned to see if I was OK and apologise once more. He said he would try to change his ways. I was very surprised, but pleasantly so. That evening I relaxed for the first time in weeks and had a full night's sleep without the aid of alcohol.

The next morning David telephoned the office. He spoke to Peter Tithe, who in addition to being the director of finance, was also the Company Secretary. I could see from my telephone who was talking to whom and how long they had been on for. David was on the phone to Peter for a very long time. I started to get the fear. Maybe David had thought some more about it overnight and now felt that after all that, he couldn't deal with me crying and in his eyes, being pathetic.

My phone rang. It was Peter. 'Hello?' I answered.

'Hello, David on line two for you'. Line two flashed at me. I so desperately wanted to pretend I was in the ladies. I picked up the call.

'Morning David.'

His voice was fine. Thank god. He asked me how I was and whether I had had a better evening, to which I replied that I had.

'Oh that's good', he replied. 'I've been having a think overnight and I'm afraid we are going to have to lose...Amy'.

I had, in a split-second braced myself to hear him say my name. My head was in a complete spin. Amy? What?

'Oh' I said.

'Yes I'm afraid she just isn't up to the job and I'm worried that she just would not be able to handle your job if you weren't here and Kathy was off sick', he said, adding that we would discuss it further when he came into the office that afternoon.

I felt sick. Poor Amy had done nothing wrong. She had worked at Arena for nearly a year. How could he just decide to get rid of her for no real reason? So what if she couldn't do *my* job? She hadn't been employed to do my job! The job that she had been employed to do was that of junior secretary and general office administrator. She was fantastic at her job. She always helped and was happy and smiley every day, despite having to deal with all the crap jobs. David was simply moving the goalposts to suit him and now that Amy didn't fit the bill, he was prepared to toss her out like an out of date food item.

I was helpless. I couldn't help but think that David had decided to suddenly make this harsh decision as some kind of a weird, underhand warning to me. It was almost as though I had annoyed David to such an extent that he had to take his anger out on someone else and I had to watch him do it.

David arrived that afternoon and called me into his office immediately. I was still prepared for him to change his mind about me any minute. Instead he talked and talked about Amy. He asked me more than once for my opinion on whether he was doing the right thing or not. I couldn't agree with him as it felt so wrong and I would have been such a traitor. On the other hand I didn't want to annoy him by being totally honest. I was still frightened of him.

It was a thoroughly strange and unpleasant exchange of words between us. All I did tell him was that for the reasons that Amy had been employed, she was excellent at her job, but if he was looking for something more, then possibly she wasn't right for *that* job. I didn't know what else to say. I also found the conversation that we had pretty pointless and merely an exercise in David pulling rank and demonstrating that he could fire who he wanted. I left his office as confused as ever. I got back to my desk and sent an email to Ed. 'I feel sick. David is about to sack Amy for no real reason and she has no idea it's about to happen.'

Amy reacted to David's sacking with utter shock and then tears. It absolutely broke my heart to see someone as lovely as Amy, crying. I don't think I had ever seen her without a smile on her face. She had been the happy person who had greeted me on my first and subsequent interviews. What was worse is that when asked what the reasons were for letting her go, David apparently had replied 'Oh, too many to go into' and Amy had simply accepted this.

She was too sweet for this place. The mood within Arena shifted to a far darker one after that day.

*

By the beginning of December, I was bursting to get out of the office. I had another three weeks until I left for the Christmas break and it could not come quickly enough. Things had calmed down dramatically between David and I. Amy had resigned herself to the fact that she was moving on and I had been busy interviewing potential new girls to take her place.

I had not sugar-coated the role in any way. I couldn't afford to. Both agents and candidates needed to know what they were letting themselves in for when they joined Arena. We had whittled the selection of candidates down to a couple. One girl I really liked as did David, but as usual, he was being slow on the recruitment process. She had already been seen three times and it was now not likely that a decision would be made until after the Christmas break.

I was kept busy up until the bitter end of what was left of the working year. It was my job to choose, order, purchase and arrange delivery for all the corporate Christmas gifts that David sent out annually. Not just in the UK either. I had to get wine delivered to the US and France. He sent mainly crates of wine, but he also sent half crates and gift hampers. It had been a mission and a half. Nina had warned me to start the planning early on because of how difficult David was about it all. He changed his mind on an almost daily basis on who should be given what. If anyone fell out of favour he took them down from a full to a half crate of wine. If he needed to suck up to someone they received a full crate plus a hamper. He was like Ebenezer Scrooge in his counting house.

By the time it came to leaving for the Christmas holiday, I had sent over sixty hampers across the UK, two hundred and sixteen bottles of Claret and organised local deliveries of wine to New York, Boston and France. All had miraculously gone to plan.

It snowed on the last week. Thankfully David was stuck down in the country for part of it. Typically, like every year that I can remember, I had developed a stinking cold just before the last working day. It always happened. As soon as my body sensed I was about to have some time off, it always allowed the colds and viruses to appear, knowing that it could lie down in a bed and not come to work. It didn't give a shit that my body actually wanted to go out and party until the small hours and drink copious amounts of mulled wine.

I said my goodbyes to my fellow workers through a haze of Vicks vapour rub. David was the last person I said my goodbyes to. He appeared rather genuine when he wished me a vigorous 'Merry Christmas'. I felt we had truly turned a corner and that I was beginning to be accepted as a vital part of the team. I left the office and walked out into a crisply cold winter's evening. I had been fantasising over this moment for months. It didn't quite feel as amazing as I had imagined, due to the fact that I was so snuffly and wanted my bed, but nevertheless it felt wonderful to be free from the drudgery for two weeks.

My Christmas was spent as usual, with my mum. Although I had a cold, it still felt amazing to be away from Fulham and David. Only when I stopped did I realise how exhausted I was travelling all that way each day and working until 6.30/6.45pm each day. Being with my mum, doing nothing but drink, eat and reminisce was blissful. I spent a week with her before heading back down south.

Ed and I never spent Christmas together because I always felt I should spend that time with my mum and equally Ed always spent time with his mum, as we had both lost our fathers at an early age. Because of this we always made sure we had a mini-break together at New Year. This year we were going to Bruges for a few nights. Unlike Christmas, I was unable to shake the feeling of dread while I was in Bruges. I didn't even realise why I was feeling the way that I was, but I was just generally depressed the whole time I was there. It was horrible. Here we were in a beautiful place with happy faces everywhere, drinking, ice-skating and generally loving life and I was on the verge of tears the entire time.

Even though I was still a good five days away from having to go back to work, I was already dreading it. More than that though, I knew that this job was just not making me happy. They could have thrown an extra twenty grand at me and I could have afforded to do more upmarket things at the weekend, bought more clothes and handbags, visited spas, had my nails done. None of it would have made me feel any better because deep down I was not satisfied with my job, nor was I at peace with myself because there was always going to be the fear that David could turn on me at any minute. That's why I couldn't enjoy my time away.

All I ended up doing was distracting myself from the thoughts. I used our hotel gym every day and bought over-priced goods that I didn't need. New Year's Eve arrived and Ed and I bought a bottle of cheap fizz and joined the hundreds of others in the main square where fireworks and music had been laid on. It was raining heavily. As midnight struck and people all around us hugged and kissed and wished each other well, the organisers played 'Happy New Year' by Abba.

I had never felt as melancholic as I did that evening.

CHAPTER TWENTY ONE

I started back at Arena on Thursday the 3rd January. I was happy that I only had to work two days before the weekend. I couldn't have done a whole week just yet. I needed to be introduced to work slowly so it wasn't so much of a shock to my system. Thankfully David was not due back in the office until the week after. It was a fairly easy start to the New Year. David got on the phone to me a few times, but he was fairly pleasant so it really wasn't as bad as I had been expecting.

One week later and Christmas seemed like a distant memory. I was back in the zone and the workload didn't feel that bad surprisingly. I think that having had the break, I had a renewed energy. David arrived on the Tuesday late afternoon as usual. He was really friendly when he saw me. He asked me all about Bruges and seemed far more jovial than I had seen him before. Maybe he had made a few New Year resolutions and being nicer to people was one of them.

It was all systems go as David had seen some flight sales for British Airways and wanted me to secure good prices for when he flew to the US later on in the year. I got on with that for the majority of my week. It wasn't an easy task as David was incredibly fussy. There was rather a lot of toing and froing, but eventually he agreed on the flights. It had taken a week to sort. I was pleased to have put it to bed. Again, as with the Christmas gifts, Nina had warned me that flights were another bane of her life because David could be such an awkward sod over them. I was so relieved that I hadn't received the amount of grief I had been expecting.

Although I had a Blackberry for work, I rarely looked at it. You might have imagined that someone like David would be the type to expect you to always be at his beck and call, 24/7, but he wasn't. He never expected you to answer outside of office hours. He spent the majority of his weekend sending emails to me and others from the office, but it was mainly as an aide-memoire for himself and he only expected you to deal with them when you got back into the office on a Monday. I had had an enjoyable weekend up until that Sunday evening. I had stupidly decided to take a look at my Blackberry at about 8pm and when I saw a bunch of emails that had been sent by David to me from the Friday evening onwards; I felt I should probably look at them.

What a bad idea that was.

I realised that not two hours after I had said goodbye to

David on the Friday evening, he had sent me a rude email accusing me of making a huge mistake in the diary for the following week. Apparently there was a clash that he could see, that I should have picked up on. As always David had completely misread the diary and not understood anything, but just jumped to conclusions and sent accusations flying. It didn't stop there.

He had gone on to find fault with practically everything and sent me three further bitchy emails on the Saturday and two on the Sunday. I was devastated. I had stupidly believed yet again, that we had turned a corner. David's emails were full of venom. Something was up. Something must have happened to have put him into such a foul mood. I was now dreading Monday all over again.

On the Monday, David called me at 9.45am. He also called me at 10.45am, 11.45am, 2.45pm, 4.00pm and 6pm. Each time he called me he had a list of things that he was not happy about. All of it was stuff that I had either done wrong in his opinion, or had failed to do entirely. If I tried to explain anything to him I was immediately cut off and told 'not to argue back'. I was battered; emotionally spent. 'Evil David' had taken the place of 'nice David' and I couldn't comprehend why. I had not done anything wrong. I was behind on nothing.

Only a week prior had he been all over me like a rash, asking me about my Christmas and New Year break and telling me just how efficient I was and he had only just thanked me once again on the Friday prior, for all of my continued hard work.

None of this behaviour made any sense. It was baffling. I went home that evening in utter despair. It seemed that there was absolutely nothing I could do. I was damned if I did and damned if I didn't.

How could I possibly continue living my life like this? How could anyone? How had Nina put up with this for six years? I felt wretched again all that evening. I was on edge all day, with an impending sense of doom. I awoke early again the next morning as I had done prior to Christmas. Anxiety about the day ahead awoke me at 4am and then 6am.

I arrived at the office on the Tuesday, feeling like absolute death. I was miserable, scared, pissed off and utterly bored of being in this unwinnable situation. Again I thought to myself, *surely* David would not say anything bad to me today? *Surely* he would know how he had made me feel the day before? I was so, so wrong.

The office phone rang at 9.30am. It was him. The call was for me. I answered. The only thing on David's mind that morning was his seat allocation on the flights to America. David had been insistent that he wanted first class and he wanted to be able to choose his seats now. I had discovered that he was not able to do this, based on his level of BA membership. Where he had once been a gold member, he was now a mere silver member and as such was not entitled to pick his seats just yet. Nor was he allowed to pay to do this, as he had suggested doing.

I had spoken to a really kind sales chap at BA, the day before and he was positive that he could do something for David. He would only be back in the office on Wednesday of this week, but with the flights being so far away, he had assured me that there would not be a problem sorting it on his return. I had sent David a detailed email the night before, explaining all of this.

It became apparent on the Tuesday morning that David had not read this email from me. He started the phone call rudely. There was something quite sinister about the tone of his voice. Again he offered no pleasantries, but got straight on with moaning.

'What are you doing about these seats' was all he offered.

'If you mean the seat allocation with BA, the sales advisor said he would get back to me tomorrow to sort this out for you' I replied.

The tempo of the conversation swiftly changed. David moved up a gear.

'I can't possibly wait until then. This is ridiculous. I need to get these seats sorted today. Why on earth didn't you do this yesterday and why are you only telling me now?'

Jesus Christ, I thought. How on earth am I going to manage this fuelled situation? I felt like a petrified animal again.

'I did send you an email yesterday about this, David. I tried to explain this to you so that you understood'. I hated these phone calls.

'I don't think you did' he accused me.

'Well, yes I did. I sent it to you before I left the office'. It was so draining to have to be defending myself first thing in the morning, but this was David all over. He didn't give a toss. He never believed anyone.

'Get the email up in front of you' he demanded. I couldn't believe the cheeky, nasty sod was not only giving me such a hard time, but he was now making me get the email up on my screen so that I could presumably read out what I had said or re-forward to him just to prove I wasn't lying.

The problem was that as usual, the internet connection had slowed right down just as I was trying to find my sent items. It only made me sound even more flustered and less-believable. As I tried meekly to explain myself, David cut me off and changed subject completely. What followed was the most bizarre conversation. There was silence for what seemed like an eternity then David spoke in what I can only describe as a sadistic tone.

David: *'Are there some problems?'*

Me: *'Sorry, I don't know what you mean, David. Problems?'*

David: *'Yes. Problems. You're under the weather, aren't you?'*

What the hell was this guy talking about? All my normal senses scrambled and I suddenly felt very odd. My face felt hot and my throat tightened. I felt like an animal being backed up into a corner with a shotgun aimed at my head.

Me: *'I'm sorry I have no idea what you are talking about, sorry David.'*

David *'Well, you've been falling behind with your work.'*

Again, I was incredulous. Utterly lost as to what he was going on about and why on earth he was suddenly spouting such utter shit. I was not behind on any of my work. He himself had only just reiterated to me that he thought I was incredibly efficient. It was as though he had gone completely mental. It was very, very frightening and incredibly upsetting, as there was just nothing I could do.

Me: *'I'm afraid I really don't know what you are talking about. As far as I am aware, I am not behind on any of my work for you, but if you believe that I am then please do let me know in which areas you think I am.'*

More silence followed. It was eerie.

I tensed as I waited for a reply. I was expecting an explosion of anger. Instead, David changed subject once more. It was like he was looking for something, anything, to pull me up on just to start a fight. I was being attacked yet again. He started talking about the diary sheets that I sent to him on a daily basis. The same diary sheets that I had been preparing for him and sending to him twice daily, in the same format for the last seven months. He had never mentioned them to me before, but suddenly he was finding fault with them and it wasn't a small thing. Now, according to him they were 'completely unacceptable'.

I think my mouth must have fallen open at this part. It was so transparent, what he was doing. I was too good for this game though and he knew it, so he was suddenly clutching at straws, trying every last dirty trick in the book trying to beat me. Beat me at what though? He needed a PA! I was his PA and, what's more, he had repeatedly told me just how good I was and yet here he was, attempting to find fault with anything he could, for seemingly no reason. I had no choice but to answer him, but as I didn't really know where this was all going, I just repeated what he had said and mid-way through talking, he snapped back at me with one of his usual lines.

'Don't argue back with me' he spat at me, and that was the final straw.

The anger within me that had been bubbling underneath had just risen to the top, like soured cream. I repeated what I had said to him on the telephone only a few months prior. I said that I couldn't do this and that I didn't understand what he was doing and I reminded him that he had promised me he would stop behaving like this, but he was doing exactly the same thing again and I felt like he just wanted to force me out of my job.

He had continued to rant at his end of the telephone all the time that *I* had been talking to him, so I am not sure what he had taken in, so I repeated it for good measure. This time tears of rage pricked my eyes and I became more animated and high-pitched and I repeated again how I felt like there was nothing more I could do and that I felt he was just trying to push me out. I told him through choked tears that I couldn't take it anymore. I was by now hysterical. Silence appeared at the moment my tears became a torrent.

David's only words to me at that moment were 'Well, you know what you can do then'.

What an utter bastard. What a complete and utter nasty piece of shit he was. Nina was right. He *was* a cunt. The biggest arsehole I had ever encountered in my entire life.

Through a mix of tears and rage I replied 'Yes, I do, because you have made it quite clear!' and I slammed the phone down into its receiver as hard as I could so it would rattle in his over-sized, old-git ears and with any luck, cause him a burst ear-drum. I was shaking with anger.

As soon as I had slammed the phone down on David a whole host of feelings rushed into my head. I felt relieved that I had once again spoken out, but then thoughts of the panic variety started to appear. What did he mean 'you know what you can do?' Did he mean walk out because I was fired? Or that I should hand my notice in? I was confused beyond belief.

Kathy and Amy came in. I told them what had happened. Everyone in the office had heard probably. I was sobbing. I felt absolutely horrendous. Of course I didn't want to work for such an asshole, but I needed time to find another job. I couldn't believe that I was in this situation. I'd only been in the job seven months and wouldn't have a leg to stand on legally, which was so bloody unfair. What if he was so angry that he wanted me out there and then? What if he held my pay back? I felt thoroughly sick. I was like a headless chicken wandering back and forth in my mind, pacing up and down the carpet in my office.

I spoke to Peter Tithe. He knew what an arsehole David was. David spoke to him like dirt more often than not, but Peter put up with it for one reason only – the money. I didn't get paid half the amount that Peter was on so there was no way I was going to be treated like a piece of shit for my salary. Peter suggested I get some air and come back ready to speak to David when he arrived that afternoon. I agreed that I needed to get out and calm down. I knew in my heart I wasn't going to be coming back to the office though, not that afternoon anyway.

I took my bag and coat and walked out into the cool winter air. It was after 11am. A reasonable enough hour to warrant buying a glass of wine without being seen as a raging alcoholic, I figured. I walked to Fulham Broadway and bought a large glass of wine.

I called one of my girlfriends. She always knew what to do. She suggested that I finish the wine I was drinking and not buy anymore. Told me to focus, eat some lunch and go back into work and confront David with a list of things I had done for him and ask him to tell me where exactly he felt I was falling behind.

My attention wandered as soon as I heard the suggestion about going back to work. There was absolutely no way I was going back to see that man today. I was far too emotional and volatile. I was in no fit state. Plus my rebellious side had now come out. I was no longer upset, I was fuming. Absolutely full of anger that yet again some tosser of a boss had decided that they could treat me like that.

Everything that my friend was saying would have been perfect advice to follow had I actually wanted my job, but I didn't. Who the hell would want a job where you get abused regularly and accused of things you haven't done or made to feel on a daily basis that if you so much as breathed in the wrong way you would get a bollocking. This was all too familiar. I needed to escape into oblivion in order to get my head together. It's what I always did and today was no exception.

I ordered another glass of wine and sent an email to David telling him that I was still too emotional and that seeing him today would be too raw for both of us so I would be taking the rest of the day off and would be in the next day. I then proceeded to get utterly annihilated on my own in three separate bars. I couldn't risk staying in the same bar as I really would have looked like a tramp. I got wasted. I veered between feeling joyfully pissed to utterly low when I ran over the scene in my head of that morning and the way David had spoken to me.

CHAPTER TWENTY TWO

The next day I awoke feeling utterly petrified of life. I couldn't do this. I sent an email to Peter Tithe telling him I was taking the day off because I had a migraine. In part this was true. I had the mother of all hangovers. I then called my doctor. I needed someone neutral on my side. I needed to hear that none of this was my fault and that it was normal to be feeling as scared as I did.

Half of me also wanted him to tell me he was signing me off work, because I just couldn't face going back. The other part of me knew that I would have to face David eventually. It was truly horrible to feel like this. I simply wanted to run away and cry. Life just felt too overwhelming. I was due to see the doctor at 3pm.

I received a phone call from the recruitment agency just before I left. I felt embarrassed talking to them. They were concerned about how I was feeling, but making noises about what I was going to do and when was I was thinking about going back into work. I wanted to scream 'I'm not going back ever. I'm going to get the doctor to sign me off and I'm going to hide in a hole until I feel better'!

I felt too embarrassed to even admit that I was thinking about getting signed off. I was paranoid that they would think I was some kind of useless flake who couldn't hack life. I lied and said I was going to speak to Peter Tithe that day and see how the land lay in the office. They said they thought it was a great idea.

I felt so lonely. I knew I couldn't run away from this. I needed to face up to it. I made a decision that I was going to go back in the next day, but I knew I would not have slept that evening without some kind of aid, because I was so scared of going back. I decided I would ask the doctor for some sleeping tablets.

Thanks to the sleeping tablets and the chat with my GP, I slept like a baby that evening. I woke with the familiar, dreaded knot in my stomach the next morning, but like so many times before, forced myself through the motions and dragged myself to the office.

I was now thinking on a different level. I needed to buy myself more time to find a new job. I needed to appeal to David's softer side. I was going to have to suck up to him. It was going to be tough and no doubt would make me want to vomit, being as false as I knew I needed to be, but this was about me and my life and I needed to do whatever was necessary.

When David appeared for the first time, he looked absolutely ashen-faced. He was clearly troubled and had not been looking forward to seeing me. It was awful. I felt acutely uneasy, but at least I knew he was feeling this too. He did not speak to me for the majority of the day and could not even bring himself to say hello to me when I acknowledged him.

At about 4pm he asked me to come into his office. He was so pale, he looked gravely ill. I think it pained him greatly to even speak to me. When he did, he said 'I'm afraid this isn't going to work'.

I replied immediately: 'You are absolutely right. This isn't going to work. I agree.' I was upbeat, friendly and mature in my demeanour.

He asked 'I wonder if you feel you might be able to work your notice?' He appeared incredibly hesitant. I knew instantly that his biggest fear had been that I was about to walk out and leave him in the lurch. This was my chance to capitalise on his fear and get what was good for me.

'David, of course I will work my notice. I wouldn't just walk out and leave you in the lurch. I will also do everything I can to ensure I find you a great replacement.' And with that, the colour returned to his cheeks.

My god, he was a true bully. In typical cowardly style, he had been brilliant at dishing the nastiness and abuse from the safety of behind a telephone, but as soon as he knew there was likely to be a face-to-face confrontation, he had become a frightened deer in the headlights. As soon as he had realised I was *not* about to continue the unpleasantness of the telephone call two days prior, he had visibly relaxed. What a chicken shit. It said it all.

I could not have been nicer to him. He even thanked me for being so good natured about it all. What did he expect?! The point was that I *was* good-natured, well-mannered and a great employee, but he had driven us to this point and for what? He was now going to lose me, even though deep in his heart he knew I was a great asset to him and that company. Thankfully as I had hoped he would, he offered the same deal to me as he had with Amy, he said to me that I could take as much time as I needed to interview and find myself a new job.

I walked back to my desk with the biggest smile on my face and I didn't even realise. It was only when I saw the girls that they told me how much I was smiling. I realised that this was the happiest I had felt in months. I was so utterly relieved that I had been given the key to unlock the door and leave this awful man behind. I was even more relieved to think that for the first time ever in searching for a job, I would be in the unique position of not having to sneak about behind my employer's back, arranging clandestine interviews. The outcome could not have been more agreeable for me.

*

What a huge difference it makes to your sense of wellbeing, when you know that you are not trapped in a job that you dislike. As soon as I knew there was light at the end of the tunnel, the weight lifted from my entire being. I was able to sleep at night and I no longer walked on eggshells. I didn't care if David was horrible to me again because I knew that he knew that none of it mattered anymore. His power had disappeared. He could no longer hold the threat of sacking me, to my throat.

For that reason, he was as nice as pie for the next few weeks. As preposterous as it seemed, even having only worked for seven months, I was still required to give two months' notice. I had thought it was a month until I received my official letter telling me otherwise. Truth be told, I was relieved. The chances of me actually finding another job within a month were slim.

I was also quite worried that no one would touch me now because my CV looked absolutely dreadful. I had gone from working at some companies for over four years to suddenly doing a stint at D&D for not even a year and a half and now one for just seven months. I knew how employer's minds worked. Well, some of them anyway. I knew that some people would only look at my most recent work history and figure that *I* was the bad penny in these scenarios.

When I thought about it, it made me angry because it was so unfair that due to two horrible bosses, I was now in this situation. I needed to just get on with it though and hope that agencies would fight my corner and explain my situation to prospective employers, in a diplomatic way.

I got back in touch with most of my old agencies. I had resisted contacting the agency who had secured the £40k job for me, which I had rejected. I felt utterly embarrassed about what had now happened and felt sure they would laugh like vengeful cartoon characters at my sudden demise. After two weeks of absolutely nothing from other agencies, I was panicking about time ticking away.

I knew I had to swallow my pride and call them. I was shame-faced. I needn't have felt so worried though. I spoke to a different lady to the one I had clearly pissed off last time. She couldn't have felt sorrier for me. Thankfully, she knew that some bosses were just utter horrors.

Then a funny thing happened. As I was describing David to her, she realised she knew all about him. Apparently Nina had gone straight to her when she was looking for a new job for herself. She had described David to her as 'an absolute shit', so at least now she knew that I was telling the truth about him. What a shame that Nina had not felt able to tell me that to my face before I ever accepted the job.

There was one job on the agency books that she thought I would be perfect for. Unfortunately it was already at the second interview stage and she was doubtful that she could get any more new people in for a first interview. She said she would try though. She told me what the job was and I was so excited, but it felt bittersweet already. I had a feeling that she wouldn't be able to get me an interview. It seemed highly unlikely that after being sent a load of first interviewees, that they wouldn't find enough to take through to a second. I was already gutted and had only just been told about the job.

The job was being PA to a very famous ex-sportsman who I will call Simon, who was very much back in the spotlight at this time, in his new role at an established sports company.

The opportunities that would open up for me seemed endless. To work for someone who was at the top of his game and an absolute living legend, seemed like a dream job. I couldn't believe that the agency I was talking to had this type of role on their radar. At the same time as being thrilled by the prospect, I was also really disappointed, because I just felt that I had missed my chance, by contacting them too late. If only I had swallowed my pride a little sooner, I might have been in with a chance.

It was no use dwelling on it though. I needed to forget pipe dreams and get on with applying for more mundane jobs if I was to continue paying my bills and keeping a roof over my head.

Over the next week, there was a flurry of activity. Aside from being similar to dating, looking for a job is also akin to waiting for a bus. You wait absolutely ages for any lead and then on one day you might get three or four roles pushed your way. To have that amount of choice buoys you. When you have zero opportunities in front of you, it can feel very depressing indeed. As soon as the phone starts to ring it's a different story. Your mood is lifted and you feel like anything is possible.

I got a phone call one particular morning from someone asking if I would be interested in a role looking after the new CEO of a well-known theatre impresario's company. I said yes to that and within half an hour I had a phone call from someone else asking me about a role working for a well-known entrepreneur at his lush offices in Mayfair. 'Yes please',

I had replied to both. There was never any point in saying no to anything at this stage, because you would never know until you had at least one interview, how you might feel about something or someone.

I was more interested in the theatre role than the entrepreneur one, but typically I got a call about the entrepreneur role first. They wanted to know if I could interview the next day, which of course I could. Apparently it would be more like a ten minute chat than an interview as really it was to decide whether they wanted me to go back and do a day or a half-day's work trial at a later stage. Interesting, I thought. I also thought what a great idea, to be able to test the water before committing.

How I was going to ask for a day or a half day off at such short notice, I didn't quite know, but would have to deal with that later. I had been given carte blanche re taking time off for interviews, but I still felt guilty about taking large chunks of time off. I still had a job to do after all and I didn't want to rock the boat, in case David decided to get rid of me before my notice was up.

I went to meet with the entrepreneur the next day. I will call him Bob. Bob is heir to a rather famous, well-established company, but the role I was being interviewed for was as his PA within the company he had started only a few years prior. His office was based on the upper two floors of a townhouse close to Bond Street. It seemed rather lovely on first impressions. I was asked to see him after a five minute wait. We both sat at a round table within his office.

He was a good-looking, charming man. I noticed that he liked to wear a lot of purple. His cufflinks, tie and socks were purple as was his writing pen. It was quite intimidating to be asked as many probing questions as I was, at such an early hour in the morning, but with only ten minutes to spare for each candidate I guessed he needed to ask as much as he could to establish whether he wanted anyone back in for the work trial.

I was the last person he was seeing that morning. We wound our chat up by approaching the current PA's desk and casually chatting about the work trial. He told me there and then he wanted me back in and for a full day, rather than just half. I felt flattered. I always did when someone was impressed enough by me to want to invite me back. He left me with the PA to arrange when this would be. I explained that I couldn't decide until I had worked out what I was going to say to David. I went back to work with a bounce in my step, hopeful that I might be able to secure myself a new job sooner than expected.

Unfortunately, there was a bit of wrangling between myself and David over the logistics of when I could do the trial. Bob wanted me in on the Friday of that week. David said he preferred it if I did the following Monday. I told them I could do the Monday as it seemed the fairest option, plus it gave me time to prepare myself. It was all agreed and as a bonus I found out that I would also be paid for the work that I did on the day's trial.

In the interim period I heard back from the theatre job

which was a 'no' as they had decided to go with someone internal. So aside from the sports marketing role, which didn't seem likely at all, this job was my only current option. I needed to make sure I went in on my game and blew their socks off next week.

CHAPTER TWENTY THREE

I arrived at the Bond Street offices at 9am. It felt more than a little odd. I hadn't been in a situation like this before. It was a very cold morning indeed, with snow swirling about. I was glad to get inside the building. I met the current PA. She was a nice person; very placid and calm, if a little lacking in personality. I would be sitting at her desk for the day. She would be sharing a double desk with the other junior PA.

Unfortunately my desk was situated in a narrow space between the larger front office that Bob used, which doubled up as a meeting room and the back office that the other PAs were sat in. Both of the larger offices had portable heaters in them. My area had no heater and was directly opposite an old-fashioned sash window, which was letting a lot of cold air in. Even on full blast, the heaters within the office did not reach as far as my desk. Unsurprisingly, I hadn't planned on it being colder in the office than out, so was only wearing a light top with a jacket. Luckily I had a pashmina with me that I was able to drape over me and tuck my cold hands up inside.

I was given 'the bible' to read. Not the actual Bible, but the big book of all things 'Bob'. Most PAs kept a book for the person they looked after. It was common practice to keep a reference of everything you need to know about looking after a certain person. i.e. what coffee they liked, favourite restaurants, dates of important people's birthdays, wedding anniversaries etc. I was asked to sit there (in the freezing cold) and read this thoroughly, as until Bob actually came into the office, there was no work for me to do. It took me less than an hour to go through the book.

Bob didn't turn up until 11.20am. I had not been shown where the ladies loos were, nor where coffee or tea was should I want to make myself a drink. In the end I was so utterly frozen that *I* had to ask where I could make a drink. I made a cup of tea just to have something to warm my hands up on.

When Bob arrived, he launched into work mode. He sat and dictated email after email into his digital recorder. At 11.40am he handed me the tape and said 'See how you get on with that lot'. The PA hadn't shown me how to use her particular type of dictation equipment, but I muddled through and made a start. At the beginning of the tape Bob said 'I'd like to see all of these as drafts first before you send them please'.

I typed away as fast as I could, but the cold air circling my desk was making it very difficult as my fingers were so stiff. It was just ridiculous that I was sitting in such arctic conditions. I was sure there was some kind of regulation that meant you weren't meant to work if the temperature was below a certain point and if so, then Bob had certainly crossed the cut-off point.

When I had done the entire tape, I printed the emails out for Bob to check, as he had requested. I then walked over to his desk with them in hand. As soon as he saw me, he looked horrified.

'Oh god no, have you printed them?' he asked.

'Yes, you said you wanted to check them before I sent them' I replied.

'No! I only wanted to check them on your screen. God, we never waste paper like that'.

Right, I thought. You could have made that clearer on the tape couldn't you, buddy? So instead of then using what I had printed, he chose to ignore that and instead marched me back to the computer and hovered behind me whilst looking at each individual email that I had done in draft. For God's sake! Why did people insist on doing this? Didn't they realise how much it put a person off?

As soon as he saw the first email I had done he balked.

'Why isn't it in purple?'

You what? Purple?!

'Erm, I didn't know you wanted it in purple?'

He shouted manically for the PA to come over to the desk, and barked at her 'Why haven't you told her how I like my emails to be done? Why haven't you told her that they need to be in the purple font?'

He was almost having a panic attack because the email was in normal black font. I was frankly too cold to give a shit. The PA didn't really have much to say apart from the fact that she hadn't shown me. She seemed to be rather tired of the whole job. It didn't bode well. He then had a paddy because the email was not set out in the way he liked it. Instead of setting out an email in the normal way with spaces and punctuation, he liked it all bunched up together.

Christ. Apart from saving paper, it was as though he needed to save virtual space too.

Then came the climax. There were three letters that the current PA had printed out ready to be sent with another document to a few people. Bob needed to sign them. I passed them to him and when he realised that none of them had a purple paper clip, he nearly self-combusted. If I hadn't felt so fricking miserable I would have laughed at how ridiculous he seemed. He signed the letters anyway on the promise that we would ensure they went out with purple paperclips. He quickly checked the rest of the emails and gave me the go ahead to send, subject to changing the font to purple.

He had a lunch to rush to so had to dash. Before he left he said to me 'Well, not the greatest of starts, was it? Shall we try and improve on it after lunch?' I smiled at him in agreement and breathed a massive sigh of relief when he departed.

The other PA came through to see me. 'How is everything? All OK?'

There was no point whatsoever in pretending.

'No. I'm afraid not' I answered as I stood to get my coat. She did not seem surprised at all. 'If I'm totally honest this just isn't for me and I don't really see the point in me doing the whole day if you aren't desperate for the help?' I continued.

She clearly wasn't rushed off her feet, he was clearly an OCD freak and I was probably going to be warmer on the street than I was in that office so it was a no brainer really. I grabbed my bag and ran as fast as my legs could carry me. What a complete waste of half a day. The only good thing was that I could spend the rest of the day at home in the warmth and continue my job search.

*

The next day, back at Arena I got a phone call from the lady about the marketing role working for the sporting legend. I had all but forgotten about it before she called. It was potentially good news. The opportunity might not be as dead in the water as previously thought.

Although they had seen a lot of first interviewees, they had not thought anyone quite right to put forward to see Simon himself. They were being quite fussy. There was now a chance that they might see me. At this stage though, my CV still had not been sent across as the agency didn't want to seem too pushy. They needed to find out what the feedback was on the last two girls before doing this.

I was impatient and desperate. I wanted to tell her to just throw caution to the wind and send it anyway, but knew that they couldn't. I would have to wait. The next three days dragged. I had only one more lead on a job, but it was for a maternity contract. Did I really want to do a maternity contract? That would only be for about nine months or a year at most and that would surely just add to my already unstable CV. It was a very frustrating time.

The only thing I had to keep my mind off it all, was arranging for candidates to come in and interview for my job, but that was bloody boring after the first few. Again, just as I was beginning to lose the will to breathe, I got a phone call on the Friday afternoon from the agency about the sports marketing role again. They had sent my CV across on the Thursday because the feedback about the last two girls was not that positive. The company had seen my CV and wanted to interview me as soon as possible.

I was so happy I could have burst. I would have seen them that evening if they had been able to, although it was a little unrealistic for a Friday. Instead we agreed on a date of the following Tuesday at midday. I would be meeting with the HR director and the lady who was Simon's business partner. I was totally up for it and started my weekend on a high for the first time in months.

I am normally great at interviews. I feel lucky that I am. I know a lot of people who hate them. They become physically sick at the very thought of attending one, long before they actually have to. I think the way I have always viewed them is as a chance to talk about me and I suppose the performer within me loves that. The interview at the sports marketing company was very different though. I felt very nervous for the first time and it was purely because of who I was potentially going to be working for. It was stupid, but I almost felt star struck and I wasn't even interviewing with Simon at this stage.

I arrived in plenty of time. I looked smart, but on trend. Not too stuffy or formal. The offices were so cool and a far cry from the boring interior of Arena Construction. There were trophies in cabinets, representing sporting achievements and framed photos of Simon himself at the peak of his own sporting career. I was in awe. This was what I wanted. This was the job for me. The environment suited me.

I was greeted first by the director of HR who was a gentle giant of a man. He could not have been lovelier or more welcoming. He walked me through the large open plan office to a meeting room where I was greeted by Simon's business partner. She couldn't have been much older than me. In contrast to him, she was a lot less friendly. My nerves kicked in massively. It was a very bright room with sunshine pouring through behind me. I was sure that beads of perspiration were gathering on my temple. I didn't dare go to wipe them away. I needed to remain composed and unflustered, whatever the circumstances.

I was first asked to run through my CV as briefly as I could, starting from the beginning. Although you probably would not have known, I was flustered inside to begin with. I had a secondary dialogue in my head, running parallel to my speaking voice. It doubted every word that was coming out of my mouth. I had to tell it to shut up. I remembered to breathe and pause and take my time so I could gather myself if I felt I was banging on too much.

I got incredibly positive reactions from the man. The woman just stayed mute, but nodded intensely every now and then and made lots of notes. After I had finished my career history, they moved on to asking me specific questions about discretion and examples of where I had worked for someone where I had needed to be discreet. It's a hard question to answer, because what I really wanted to say was 'Well, I just *have* been discreet otherwise I would have been sacked'.

There isn't really a secret formula to being discreet. You either are or you aren't. It was a pretty silly question. Nevertheless, I answered it and they both appeared satisfied with my answer. Then I was done. The interview was over. The obligatory 'Do you have any questions for us' was asked. I answered with the usual 'How long do you expect the recruitment process to take?' They told me that they were looking to make a decision as soon as they could, but it had to be the right candidate so were prepared to wait.

They made a strong point of telling me that out of all of the candidates they saw, they would only ever put two people in front of Simon. Gulp. I wondered if I had done enough to warrant being given that honour. I said goodbye to both of them and told myself that the reason why she had been cagier was that she knew Simon more than anyone and was probably silently scrutinising me and my mannerisms.

I called the agency as soon as I was out of the office and told them that I thought it had gone as well as it possibly could. I genuinely did feel that I couldn't have given any more of myself in the interview. They either liked me or they didn't.

*

I got back to my office at about 1.30pm. As it was a Tuesday, David wasn't in the office just yet. I kept my mind occupied with trawling through CVs that had been sent in for my position. Aside from using agencies, David had always insisted on placing a large half page advert in *The Times* whenever he was advertising for a role.

I remembered from when I had been interested in the role myself and had seen one then. It cost a pretty penny and didn't really get any good results. Without the filtering that an agency would normally do, an ad in a newspaper simply harvested everything including the good, the bad and the absolute worst applications. It was novel to begin with and after the first hundred applications it became painful.

I had CVs sent to me from India, Newcastle, Birmingham and Germany. All of these applicants had insisted that although they didn't actually have anywhere to live in London, they would definitely start looking for somewhere if they were offered this job. It wasn't even worth my time looking at their experience or qualifications. David wouldn't touch anyone who didn't already live within an hour's commute of the office, so there was no way on earth he would even look at any of these applicants.

I binned a hefty amount of CVs before finding anyone even remotely suitable and by then I was bored of looking at them. I kept wondering about the interview and wondering how I had done. I had already been warned by the agency that they absolutely took their time so I wasn't expecting an answer anytime soon, but couldn't help but daydream. In the middle of my daydream, my phone rang. I hadn't even heard the main office phone, so presumed it was just internal, but it wasn't, it was David. By now it was 2.40pm. I took the call.

David was calling me from his car phone, which I hated because aside from every phone call from him being awkward anyway, from his car it was even worse as I could never hear what he was saying to me. Just as he was getting into full flow, my mobile phone started to ring. It was set to silent, but was facing up on my desk. It was the agency about the sports company job. I recognised the number. I was absolutely gagging to answer my phone, but had to keep listening to David wittering on. He kept me talking for a good five minutes about nothing in particular. Bloody typical.

I kept looking at my phone expecting to see notification that a voice message had been left. I didn't get one. When David finally let me go, I immediately logged onto my personal email account. There was a new email from the agency asking me to call them. My stomach flipped. I had a feeling it was good news. I called back straight away.

'Thanks for calling back' they said. 'We just wanted to let you know that you smashed it. They absolutely loved you and thought you would be perfect for the job and they want to get you in front of Simon as soon as possible'. I was thrilled! It was the best news. To think I had thought the opportunity dead in the water just a few days prior and now I was about to go and meet him.

Simon was a very busy guy so the interview with him would not be until the week after. I opted for the earliest of all the options I had been given, which meant the following Wednesday at 6pm. The agency was impressed. They had not known them to turn around as quickly as they just had done from first interview to even feedback before, let alone arranging for anyone to actually see Simon himself. Maybe finally this was what I needed; to work for someone well-known, prestigious and respected. Someone who wasn't necessarily a business person first. Yes, this felt more and more like me.

Even if I went ahead with the interview and I still didn't get the job, I was bowled over to think I was even going to be in the same room as this person, breathing the same air. I spent that evening and the following days looking at YouTube clips of Simon at his peak. I watched footage of old interviews and more recent ones.

I was trying to work out whether he seemed like a nice guy or a complete horror. Just because he was famous didn't mean he would be any nicer than anyone else and I needed to know that I would like my next job. It was silly to try and judge from old and new footage though. All I was looking at was his media face, which wouldn't tell me a thing. I was going to have to try and suss him out at interview.

In amongst looking for a job, I was of course busy trying to recruit someone to do my job. I had been as honest as I could be with both agents and candidates. Some agencies got it – they had only sent me people who were tough and used to dealing with nasty bosses and for some reason beyond my own comprehension, didn't seem to mind them. Others had foolishly sent me girls who were as timid as the day was long.

On the day I was due to see Simon I had two interviews planned. The first was with a girl who had worked with the same man for the last nine years. She seemed incredibly bright and was very well presented. She only lived about a five minute walk away from the office, which I knew would be a big bonus for David. Job-wise she had everything that we were looking for. What mattered most was whether she could handle David. There was no way I was going to paint the picture anything other than truthfully. I couldn't allow myself to let anyone blindly walk into the lion's den. They needed to know exactly what they were getting themselves into.

I explained how David was in as much detail as I could. Nothing seemed to faze the first girl at all. She was confident that none of this behaviour would bother her. In her words, it was nothing she hadn't handled before. I was impressed. She wasn't cocky at all. Cocky would not have gone down well with David. She was quietly confident though. I felt she had a core of steel running through her which is exactly what was needed and precisely what I didn't have – or perhaps I was just too old to be bothered with now.

The second interview of the day was altogether more tragic. I interviewed a lovely lady who looked a little odd.

She had painted on her eyebrows, but they were slightly uneven and I couldn't help but keep looking at them. I went through the usual questions about why she wanted the job, what she had done before, where she lived and what her ideal boss would be like. So far, so good. I then got onto the subject of what she wouldn't like in a boss. Her first answer was 'I wouldn't want to work for a bully. I wouldn't want to work for someone who made me fearful of coming into my job because they upset me'.

I was rather flummoxed. Why the hell had the agent sent me this person? There was absolutely nothing wrong with not wanting these things in a job – no one in their right mind should want them; but I had clearly indicated that David was exactly this type of person, so I could not understand why had they sent me this candidate?

I decided not to go too far down the truth route with her. There wasn't any point because her answer had told me everything I needed to know. I simply indicated that David could be challenging and we left it there. I felt exhausted after I said goodbye to her. I still had a few things to finish before making myself look more presentable for my interview. It was finally time for me to win over one of Britain's ultimate sporting legends, and at the very least, I mused, I'd like my eyebrows to be in order.

CHAPTER TWENTY FOUR

I arrived back at the sports company with a good ten minutes to spare. I sat on one of the huge colourful sofas that sat in the reception. It wasn't until 6.10pm that Simon's business partner made an appearance. She apologised, but Simon was running late. She made me a cup of tea and sat me in a different, more out of the way area. It was 6.30pm before she came back to take me through to meet him.

I was more excited than nervous. I saw him in the distance inside a glass-walled office. A small thrill ran through me. There he was in full 3D! I couldn't believe I was about to have an interview with him. I hovered inside what was his office until he walked in. He was smaller than I had imagined. Handsome though, and very smiley. He shook my hand firmly and motioned for me to sit. He told me he was hugely flattered that *I* wanted to work for him, which I found ever so slightly disingenuous. Nevertheless I let him waffle on for a bit longer.

He didn't pick up my CV once, even though it was sat on the table in front of him. I was lost for most of the interview because he didn't ask me any of the normal questions that you would expect. He merely chatted on about random things such as his children and then finally half way through he actually asked me what my background was and where I had worked previously. I wasn't able to expand much on this though as he went off on a tangent once more and we were suddenly talking about jazz music.

It was all very lovely, but I didn't get any sense that he was at all concerned about my credentials. I could only surmise that he trusted his aids so implicitly that he knew that they would not have put me in front of him, had they not thought me capable of actually doing the job. I could have only been with Simon for a total of about ten minutes. He seemed momentarily distracted just before we finished and then he suddenly clapped his hands together enthusiastically and said

'Right, well I suppose you should really meet my wife next'. I was amazed. Was the job mine?

It felt as though my meeting with him had merely been a formality and that he had already made his mind up that I was the person for the job, but that he just had to meet me to check I didn't have two heads first. I could not bloody believe it. I was on cloud nine. I stood up and as I did, his business partner came in. She got my coat for me and, as I was busy getting myself together, she told Simon that the Prime Minister had telephoned and would he please call him back.

Simon raised his eyebrows to me and said 'You see? this is the kind of thing you'll need to deal with' and laughed. I guffawed with him as though we were now on the same team. What fun this was going to be.

I grabbed my bag and as I went to say goodbye to Simon, it was as though someone had turned the lights off. He was sat down busying himself with some papers. I thought he would have at least stayed standing and shown me out with a hand shake and a 'Welcome aboard' type look. Hmm.

I offered my goodbye to him and he looked up as if having been interrupted and for a split-second he seemed not to have a clue who I even was.

'Ah yes, bye then' he said, and immediately he looked back down at his papers. It was the second thing that had made me question his sincerity. Nevertheless I left the building, still giddy and immediately called my mum to tell her all about having met Simon.

I awoke the next day feeling like I probably had the job in the bag, but also like there was something not quite right at the same time. All the signs had pointed to me being the winner, but as I hadn't actually heard the words 'We'd like to offer you the job', I couldn't presume I had even reached the finish line. I was excited about having met Simon at all and I think this was slightly clouding my feelings. It was certainly an odd feeling.

I couldn't wait to get to work and call the agency and see what feedback they had received, as that was probably going to be my gauge. Everybody asked me how the interview had gone when I arrived at the office. I was full of glee, telling them that we had chatted about jazz music and his children and that he had said I was to meet his wife next! No one could believe it. They all said the job *must* be mine.

I went to my own office, closed the door and called the agency. I was put on speaker phone so that the whole agency could hear about the interview. They were as excited as my colleagues had been. They expressed disbelief that I hadn't actually been offered the job at the interview itself, but felt sure that it would be great news before the morning was through. I was so thrilled. It wasn't a yes yet, but it was as good as.

I had to conduct an interview that morning. I could not have been chirpier. I was full of the joys of spring. I kept getting tingles every time there was a slight lull in the interview and my mind wandered to what might be and I couldn't wait to get back to my office and check my phone for messages. When the interview was over I hurried back and saw that I had had a missed call and a voice message was waiting for me. My heart leapt. I immediately listened to the message, but it was from another agency confirming that I had been asked to attend an interview for another maternity contract. I ignored it.

By 11.45am, I had yet to hear about the job. Doubts started to creep in. I knew how this game worked. I had done it too many times. If someone wants you, they make it known. There is no game-playing and no hesitation. It's the same as in romance. When you know, you know. You don't have to make excuses for why they haven't called or start trying to second guess. I waited until midday and then I sent an email to the agency. Within minutes I had a reply. Apparently another candidate had appeared from the woodwork at the last minute and so they were now considering her.

I should have known it was too good to be true. How could someone have appeared suddenly between me having met Simon the night before and a few hours of the next day? My agency was livid. I think they thought the job was mine even more than I did.

I was so disappointed. I really wanted to know what had happened and who this person was. They said they would try to find out. On the plus side, HR loved me apparently and asked to let me know that I had not put a foot wrong. It was comforting to hear feedback, but it wasn't what I wanted to hear.

I was absolutely gutted. It wasn't perfect and in my heart I knew it never would be.

*

I was made to wait another two weeks before I finally got confirmation that the job with Simon had gone to another candidate. I was very much kept in the dark the majority of that time. Not by my agency, but by the sports company. They messed us all about.

Why on earth had Simon indicated that I had the job? Why had he said I should meet his wife? Didn't he care that words like that were dangerous? Words like that got my hopes up. He just didn't care though did he? What was I to him? As long as he still lived his life and absorbed all the adulation, he was OK, wasn't he?

My opinion on Simon changed dramatically that day. He was no longer the great hero I had imagined.

The head of HR tried to keep me interested by dangling a carrot. They told the agency that there was another job within the company that would actually pay more – that they thought I would be perfect for – but that hadn't been signed off yet. I didn't actually expect that opportunity to ever come to fruition (and it never did). I was so disillusioned by now that I didn't really care either. I was now very worried that as I had wasted such a lot of time hoping that the Simon job would come good, I had not been trying as hard for other opportunities and the reality was that I now had to get *any* job if I was to be able to afford to live.

We were also now at second stage interviews for my job at Arena, which was rather disconcerting. The only good thing in all of this was that things had been going well between David and I. Ironically, we had been working really well as a team. Peter Tithe had been sniffing about a lot in recent days, asking me how the job search was going. I hadn't realised at the time, but he had been testing the water on behalf of David. It was the last thing I had wanted to hear, having felt so rubbish about the whole Simon scenario, but David appeared in my office one afternoon looking sheepish. I knew that look. He had nothing to apologise for this time, so it meant he wanted something.

I knew before he said it, what he was going to say. He said that it seemed so silly that I was leaving, as we were getting on so well. He remarked that I had been so smiley and happy over the last few weeks. (I wanted to say 'Of course I have been happy. I have been happy ever since you asked me to work my notice. I'm happy because I know I'm getting out of here!'). And then it came: he asked me if I would like to continue working at Arena.

My heart sank. He said he would drop the recruitment drive if I agreed and we could carry on as if nothing had happened. I had known this was going to happen. I knew he would regret his behaviour and ask me to stay. I felt nauseous. I did not want to stay working for him. I hated working for him and I was desperate to get out, but at the same time I had been bitterly disappointed about other job opportunities and I was beginning to feel desperate. I was flattered, as always, that even after all the crap we had been through, he still wanted me to stay. I also felt incredibly guilty because despite everything, I was a nice person and here was a stubborn guy in his mid-seventies, swallowing his pride and asking me to stay.

I couldn't accept though. I just couldn't do it as I knew I would feel utterly wretched if I downed tools and just stayed on there. Too much had happened. I also now hated the area where I worked as it was so boring. There was nowhere to go at lunchtime. There was no fun in the office. David would revert to type as soon as I agreed to stay on and I just did not want to do this anymore. Ironically, after all that happened, it was still an incredibly tough thing to have to say no to keeping my job, but I took a leap of faith and did it. I wondered if I would live to regret my decision, but I felt nothing but relief as soon as it was done, so I knew it was the right move. Once that door was finally closed, it was full steam ahead on getting my replacement.

The girl who I had liked all along and who only lived five minutes away, was brought back for a third interview. I had a feeling she would be offered the job. I was almost at the point of resigning myself to having to temp when I left Arena, when my friend Jackie got in touch about a possible PA role.

Jackie had been my friend since college. She had recently married a guy who was lead singer with a Dutch band and they had decided to make the move to Holland with a view to him trying to crack the music scene over there (he was the only Brit in the band). She had been temping herself, for a lady called Bonnie who owned a recruitment company and was only going to be there for the next three weeks before leaving for Holland. She told me that Bonnie was looking for a permanent PA, but she was only paying up to £35k. I said there was no way I could drop as low as that, thanked Jackie for the thought and left it at that.

However, two days later Jackie got in touch again and said she had been talking at length with Bonnie and had convinced her that the way forward was to hire a more expensive PA because she needed a long-term, quality assistant. Bonnie wanted to meet with me if I was interested and she was prepared to up the salary for the right person. I couldn't have been more grateful to Jackie. Perhaps fate was going to step in at the right moment after all.

I met Bonnie one morning at her offices. It felt strange, as the recruitment company she owned was one that I was already signed up to. They had never been very proactive on my behalf in the past though. My interview had been arranged for 9am, but Bonnie only appeared at 9.20am. She was a big ball of flustered hot air and hugely apologetic for being late. She wore a tight skirt, leopard-print blouse and patterned black tights with huge stilettoes. Her hair was blonde and over-sized. It was blow-dried to within an inch of its life and it was clearly not her natural colour. I even wondered if it was a wig.

Bonnie was in her fifties, but dressed like a dolly bird. She was incredibly sweet and kind, but didn't stop talking or wandering off subject. By the end of our meeting I knew all about her divorce, which had been incredibly acrimonious and she had told me about a long-term colleague who she had just taken to court for trying to steal her clients. Bonnie seemed like a bit of a mess and I thought she really did need someone like me to organise her. She'd only ever had young juniors looking after her, which is why things had gone wrong and she had gone through so many of them. Had my friend not been working for her, I probably would have had alarm bells going off at this information, but I trusted Jackie's judgement.

Bonnie kept me talking for about an hour and ten minutes. I couldn't believe it was 10.30am when she finally let me out. David would not be happy that an interview had taken this long. I felt sure that she liked me though and I was positive I could do the job and help her. I hurried back to my office feeling a bit more positive about the future. As predicted, David was grumpy when I got back. He called me into his office and asked me to ensure that I only booked interviews at the beginning and the end of the day in future. I explained that I *had* arranged this particular interview for an early start, but that I had been kept talking for way over an hour. He said rather sarcastically he hoped it had been worth it. I couldn't have agreed more.

I got word from Jackie later that day that Bonnie had squealed with delight when she knew I was interested in the role. Jackie and I had spoken privately straight after the interview and Bonnie had asked her to find out subtly what my thoughts were. She wanted me to come back at the end of the week to see her again. I didn't quite understand why. She had had a very long time with me that morning. Apparently there were some tests that she wanted me to complete first though. Perhaps it would be to discuss the results, I thought.

The tests that she wanted me to complete were the ones that give you multiple choice answers to various questions. The results are meant to tell someone what type of a worker you are. i.e. honest, hard-working, manipulative, selfish etc. I was more than happy to do these. They at least would keep me busy in between doing David's work, which was by now, really beginning to drag. It took me a while to complete the tests as David, rather annoyingly, kept interrupting me with incredibly tedious questions. Once finished there was nothing I could do. Bonnie would receive the results immediately and I would never know whether they indicated I was psychotic, manic or an over-helpful worker. It was all in the lap of the gods.

I was due to see Bonnie in two days' time on a Friday. I was hoping that she would make a decision on the same day because I was due to fly to Barcelona on the Saturday, for a long weekend, and knowing that I had a job in the bag would really give me the boost that I needed and prevent me from feeling too guilty about spending money that I potentially might not have. My fingers and toes were firmly crossed.

CHAPTER TWENTY FIVE

Bonnie was on time for my second interview, thank goodness. I don't think David would have been as understanding, had I been late again and I really couldn't be doing with the grief from the miserly old git. Instead of chatting in her office as we had last time, she asked me into the boardroom which I thought was perhaps a sign that she was going to offer me the job that morning. We sat down and instead of her being the chatty and slightly ditzy blonde she had been previously, she was rather more business-like.

Her personality had shifted ever so slightly, but I couldn't put a finger on what was wrong. Maybe the results of my personality test had been awful and some hidden, hideous traits of mine had been unearthed through the power of multiple-choice?

She was very serious indeed. It made me feel slightly

uncomfortable and I found myself wondering whether this really wasn't for me after all. The test wasn't mentioned at all. Instead Bonnie kept asking how efficient I was and whether I could really work speedily and accurately? She seemed to be concerned that even though my CV said I could and *I* was saying I could, how could she actually *believe* that I would? I did my best to reassure her and used examples from past jobs where I had been under pressure and yet still pulled a rabbit out of the hat. It seemed to placate her.

She became less frosty and more smiley then. Something still wasn't right though. I felt it, but again I could not work out what it was. We parted company and Jackie showed me to the door. I felt uneasy on the way back to the office. If this wasn't right for me then what was I going to do? Time was running out. As it stood I was due to complete my notice period in a couple of weeks. There was of course every chance that David would increase it, because we hadn't actually offered my job to anyone as yet, but there was no guarantee on this, which made me very anxious indeed.

I arrived back in the office and got on with the usual drudgery. I tried contacting Jackie to see if she had any indication on what Bonnie was going to do next. This time Jackie was not coming back to me. I didn't understand why. Had I done something hideously wrong in the interview? My entire morning and early afternoon was dominated with negative, worrisome thoughts. Nothing settled me.

*

Finally that afternoon I had a phone call.

'Hi, it's Bonnie'.

The number had not come up, but instead, Unknown had flashed on my screen. Her voice was very sing-song. She seemed to be in a good mood. It was 4pm. 'I'm sorry it's taken me a while to get back to you. I had to attend a board meeting followed by another client meeting, but I really wanted to contact you earlier. I wanted to say I really enjoyed meeting you again today and I'd really like to offer you the job'. Oh my lord, just in time. I was relieved. I had a job to go to. It was slightly underwhelming as a job-offer, but it was better than a rejection.

Bonnie wanted me to start sooner than I had anticipated. I knew I couldn't do when she wanted though. It meant that I would only have time to do a short handover even if my job was offered to someone soon. I was going to have to do some serious negotiating with David. If I worked until my official notice period was done, I would be able to offer him a week of training the new person, but nothing more. I was already cowering inside as I practiced telling David.

I had to do what was right for me though, and this was at least a compromise, besides I could have officially walked out as soon as my notice was up anyway, so I technically didn't owe him a thing, especially after the way he had treated me.

It wasn't long before David appeared in my office. I needed to sort this all out before I went away for the weekend. He must have been reading my mind because he asked me how my job search was going. I told him I'd just accepted a job.

I then had to tell him my proposals for a handover with whoever he picked as my replacement. He did not take it well at all. He visibly got more and more wound up like a firework ready to explode as his brain comprehended what I was actually saying.

Instead of me staying silent as I had in the past, and without a telephone for him to hide behind, this was different. He didn't like that I was answering him back, one little bit. I had to though. It wasn't fair. He was accusing me of being selfish for dropping him in it. I couldn't believe the cheek of it! He was the arsehole in this scenario, not me. He tried to shut me up by saying he wasn't going to argue, but it wasn't working this time because I had nothing to lose. I would have walked that day if he'd pushed me enough and he knew it. I told him I was at least offering a solution and that I could more than show someone the ropes in a week. He stormed off, knowing that there was nothing he could do.

It had been thoroughly unpleasant to have to go through this again with him. It had also completely removed any last traces of shine from my job offer. I knew I would have to let Jackie know that there was potential for me not being able to start with Bonnie as early as I thought. What a mess it all felt. I was shaking from the fallout of my argument with David, but more than that I was fuming with him. I sent Jackie an email.

From: V Knowles
Sent: Friday 16:43 PM

To: *******
Subject: Christ
My boss is being a nightmare. Almost had a stand-up row with him. He says I need to give notice and do at least a 2 week handover blah blah blah. Talk about souring the mood. I just offered to do a week's handover or come back in my own time to help train the new girl. He is being an utter tosser, saying I'm not fair and then said 'oh it suits you now because you've got a new job' blah blah – what a cunt. I'm wound up now. My hands are shaking x

I was really worried about seeing David again. I just wanted the day to end and for him to keep out of my way until I could leave the office and go to Barcelona to forget it all. That was not going to happen though. I saw David shuffling towards me. He started taking before he was even inside my office. 'So what are you suggesting then? That you do one full week's handover?' He had obviously mulled it over and was now a bit calmer. I didn't want it to be awkward. There was no need. I was really pleased he seemed to be compromising. He left my office and I thought I would tell Jackie what the latest was and that it might not be as bad as I had first thought.

I wondered why she hadn't already replied to my last email though, which was still sitting on my screen in the sent items. I then noticed something that made my heart stop.

I hadn't sent my email to Jackie.

I had sent it to David.

I wanted the entire earth to swallow me whole there and then. I went into complete panic mode. What the fuck had I sent it to David for? I had never, ever made a mistake as grave as this in my entire working career, so why had my brain decided to betray me now? His name was nowhere near Jackie's in my address list. I must have been so wound up by him after our argument that he was quite simply on my brain.

I quickly checked his inbox – it was sitting there in all its unread glory. I deleted it immediately. I knew that he would still have it on his Blackberry though. I remembered that anything deleted from the desktop PC still remained on that until you decided to delete it manually.

I was still pretty much fucked.

My only hope was that David had left his Blackberry on his office desk as he sometimes did. I hurried along the corridor. His door was ajar so I popped my head in to find he was not there. I was frantically trying to find his Blackberry when I heard his footsteps coming towards his office. My heart sank. I had to own up. Like a plaster that had been on too long, I needed to rip it now and rip it good.

'Oh, hello.' said David, a little surprised to find me in his office.

'Hi David. I was looking for you as I need to tell you something.'

David was intrigued. I continued 'Erm yes, well… After our argument I sent an email about you to my friend Jackie and it was rather rude, but I discovered that I didn't send it to her. I sent it to you, by mistake'

'Oh dear' he said rather bemused. 'What did it say' he asked.

'Well I called you a tosser in it, I'm afraid. I'm really sorry.' I offered.

At that moment, I genuinely had forgotten that I had also used the C word. The word 'tosser' had stood out on the screen when I had realised my gargantuan mistake and I had not waited around to read the rest of it. David, to be fair, didn't react as badly as I had expected. I could have sworn he also had a little laugh just before he replied and said 'Oh well, at least I know now' and shuffled off past me, out of his office.

It was only when I got back to my desk and re-read what I had sent, that I realised my omission. I wanted to die. It was the most horrible feeling in the world. I was also incredibly pissed off that up until that point, I had held the moral high ground and now I had lowered myself to his level.

It was one of the worst working days I had ever had.

CHAPTER TWENTY SIX

I was queuing for passport control at Southend Airport when I felt my work Blackberry buzz into life. I had had it switched off for the flight back from Barcelona, but now it was manically delivering emails all at once. The queue was very slow-moving so I looked at my inbox wondering if I had been sent anything more interesting than the usual ranting from David.

There was an email from Bonnie asking me to please send her my personal email address so she could send me some more tests. I sent it to her straight away. She replied instantly to say thanks and asked if I would like to have lunch with her the following week before I started. How nice, I thought. We spoke about possible dates and she said she would confirm on my personal email. She also explained that the tests were nothing to worry about. They were just the usual admin tests and it was simply procedure as she needed to have the results on file.

I did think it odd that she was asking for them to be done now, considering I had been offered and had accepted the job, but I knew that she had to be extra careful in doing things by the book recently, due to her colleague having done the dirty on her. At least things were still progressing and having a lunch with Bonnie was a really nice idea and very thoughtful of her.

I started back at work on the Wednesday, feeling refreshed after my weekend away. I was slightly tentative about seeing David for the first time since email-gate. I needn't have been. He was full of beans when he saw me. I wondered if it was the same person. It was very disconcerting. He informed me that he had offered my job to the girl who lived five minutes away and she had accepted.

I felt the tiniest of twinges when he told me. I presume the feeling was jealousy. Ridiculously I felt pissed off about the fact that my job was no longer my job. My lovely fifty thousand pounds a year was now going to line someone else's pockets, while I was about to go off and do another job for ten thousand pounds less. It hurt. I knew it was for the best though. I suppose I was happy that it was all finally coming to an end. The timing could not have been better had I planned it. I had a week left before new girl started, then I would have a week training her before I started with Bonnie. I was pleased that the living nightmare of working for David was coming to an end.

I checked my personal emails mid-morning and had been

sent the tests by Bonnie. I wanted to get them out of the way so cracked on with them before lunch. I didn't take them entirely seriously as I knew it was just a formality. I hated these tests anyway. I got sent tests in PowerPoint, Excel, Word and typing.

What I hated about them was that you could so easily fail on a point if you didn't do what the test expected you to do, based on its set of rules. The problem was that I had my own way of doing things and each programme usually had shortcuts that most people used, including me. When it came to testing, I had forgotten what the official way of answering certain questions was and using shortcuts automatically gave you a fail. When it came to the typing test, it simply meant copy-typing the extract of text that was provided and it was timed to five minutes. I got interrupted more than once whilst attempting to complete this, but still typed as fast and as accurately as I could in the time allowed. I didn't see my results. They got sent directly to Bonnie.

I sent her a brief email to tell her I had done the tests and ask about the lunch date. She replied and could not have been more gushing. She said how thrilled she was that I was starting and she felt that we would work well together. I felt the same. We confirmed a date for the following week, which meant I would have to abandon the new girl one lunch, but didn't really care at this point.

After lunch I took an unexpected phone call from one of the agencies I was registered with. I hadn't heard from them in a while and hadn't even thought to tell people I was off the job market yet. They had a role on that they were keen to get me interviewed for. I thanked them profusely, but explained that I had a new job. I don't know why, but when they asked me where I was going to be working I was embarrassed about admitting I would be working for the owner of a recruitment company, even though they were one! Recruitment companies had a bad reputation and I felt like I was somehow selling my soul by moving into this field.

When I did tell them who exactly I would be working for, the response I got was one that I wasn't expecting. There was almost silence, like I had told a really politically incorrect joke at a dinner party. The person who had called me wasn't my usual contact or the person I had originally signed up with, but suddenly I was being asked to hold on while they put them on the phone to talk to me. I just knew what was coming and I didn't want to hear it.

'Hi, I hear you are off to work for Bonnie?' She asked.

'Yes I was offered the job last week, so it has happened just in time… Lucky me!'

I tried to make it sound light and fun. I wasn't feeling light and full of fun though. I was suddenly worried what she was about to say to me as I could sense in her voice that something was not right.

'Oh dear, are you sure this is the right move for you? I do feel that perhaps you will be jumping from the frying pan into the fire. I mean I don't know her personally, but she's got a bit of a reputation as being quite difficult and she does tend to get through PAs quickly'.

Hearing this was just awful. Why was she telling me this? I had accepted the job already. My friend had been working for Bonnie for the last few weeks and hadn't told me any horror stories about Bonnie. I had met with her twice and for lengthy periods of time. Surely my judgement, coupled with Jackie's, was enough? Maybe the agency were just hacked off that I wasn't going to go to this interview and all they really cared about was their commission? Yes, that was it. It was sour grapes. I chose to ignore what she was saying and said I was grateful for them thinking of me, but that I had made my mind up and thought that Bonnie was really nice and that I wasn't interested in interviewing for their role.

I started to wonder though, whether I was trying to convince myself as much as I was them. Even if I did now have doubts, what could I do? I had to earn money and I needed a job. I would have to see it through and hope that it was for the best.

I felt uneasy for the rest of the day. Was it my conversation with the rival agency about Bonnie or was it something more deep rooted? I was incredibly busy trying to tie up loose ends before the new girl started, but I was finding it difficult to concentrate. I was busily filing documents that I had put off doing for weeks when my mobile rang. It startled me as I had forgotten to switch it to silent. It was an unknown number calling. I had a feeling it was Bonnie. I chose to ignore it. Something inside me didn't want to take the call. I sensed something was wrong. I know it sounds ridiculous, but there really were bad vibes in the air. I waited for the voice message indication. When it popped up on screen, I paused for quite a while before listening to it. The voice was Bonnie's.

She was her usual breezy-voiced self. 'Hi there! It's Bonnie. Would you be able to call me please when you get this message? Can you call me on my Blackberry number not the office number? OK. Thanks'. I couldn't tell a thing from her message. Her voice was suitably upbeat for it not to be anything bad, but at the same time why did she want to talk to me?

I had to just bite the bullet.

I closed my office door, sat back down at my desk and dialled her number. She answered straight away. I sounded as enthusiastic as I could, even though I was feeling distinctly worried by now.

'Hi Bonnie!' I chirped down the phone.

Bonnie's voice, when she spoke, had changed. Oh fuck, fuck, fuck. What was wrong? Something was wrong.

'Hi. Thanks for calling me back. Yes, I've been looking at your test results and they're not great and it's rather worrying if I'm totally honest'. Silence.

What the fuck? I couldn't believe my ears. I thought it was a joke. I heard my own voice making light of it

'Oh dear,' I said with a slight chuckle. This was not funny to Bonnie.

'Yes, I really am worried now, I have to say. The scores you got across the board weren't advanced at all and your typing was only fifty words a minute and I'm really looking for someone who can type at about seventy five words a minute.'

My face went red as she continued to slate my abilities,

but more than that I knew that she was backing out of the deal. She didn't want me. She had changed her mind like an utter lunatic. What happened to being thrilled at me working with her? What about our lunch? The date had been agreed! I could have fought. I could have tried to defend myself and explain that I didn't actually try at the tests because I didn't think they mattered. I could have explained that my typing is faster than that, but that I got interrupted by David.

I couldn't be arsed though. Bonnie was revealing more and more in this one phone call than in any interview and I was freaking out at what an utter weirdo she had suddenly become. Not once had she specifically mentioned that she needed someone to type as fast as seventy five words a minute. This was a speed reserved for medical and legal secretaries. I was about to be a PA for the owner of a tin-pot recruitment company, for fuck's sake! I didn't need to type that quickly!

My CV also spoke for itself – I had been a PA for some pretty prestigious people. I had done a fantastic job for them and could provide references saying so. I needed a job, but I didn't need this one. She did everything but rescind her offer. She said she would sleep on it and get back to me the next day. I changed tack and suddenly became super understanding of Bonnie's dilemma. I wanted to get her off the phone and not have a row. I told her it was entirely up to her and that I would wait patiently for her decision. We ended our call. What a fucking nutjob she was.

I was in shock. You literally couldn't have written this. I was on a white rapids ride of utter catastrophe. Nothing was working out for me. I could not believe that someone in her line of work could be so unprofessional and start querying my skills, having interviewed me twice and offered me the job already! I didn't know whether to laugh, cry or go round to Bonnie's office and go absolutely ballistic at her. What a stupid, stupid woman. I was absolutely fuming.

I started to type an email to her. I wasn't going to send it straight away, but I had to get my rage out and on paper. I went through a couple of edits before settling on what I was going to send to her, but I decided to sit on it overnight before sending to her the next day. I was curious to see what she would actually say to me in the morning.

I waited most of the morning simply out of curiosity, to see if Bonnie was going to get back to me as she had promised. I heard nothing. In the end I couldn't be bothered waiting for her. She was one silly cow and I needed to tell her. I sent the email.

From: v********
To: bonnie.m****@*****co.uk
Subject: Your Job Offer to me
Bonnie.
I feel it would be too awkward to speak with you on the telephone and as I have yet to receive the call that you promised me, I thought it best to nip this situation in the bud before you make that call.

Your call yesterday floored me. To say I was shocked to receive it is an understatement.

It is safe to say that you and I would not work well together after all if the real you is in fact the person who called me. I actually believed that the lady I met for a two hour interview and a subsequent 1.5 hour interview was the person I would be working with and as such I was excited and willing to drop £10,000 in salary in order to come on board and really help someone who I genuinely believed needed and would benefit from my PA expertise.

Instead what I believe came across yesterday was someone who micro-manages and whose standards are such that, in reality, the only person who would ever help you would be a carbon copy of yourself who is able to type at 90wpm and score 100% in faceless computer tests.

In my experience, and from the insight of many other recruitment agencies that I am in touch with, being able to type at that speed is only really a prerequisite of legal and medical secretaries.

Forgive me, but I believed that you were looking for a Personal Assistant to help run your life while you went out to find more business and grow your company further. A Personal Assistant is much more than a typist. I am a typist who actually types at about 55 to 60 wpm – perfectly adequate for a PA. I also scored good percentages in PowerPoint and Word – more than is required to be capable of doing a PA job well. At no stage was it mentioned to me that you required anything above this.

I have worked for some of the most demanding and high achieving, successful people out there in my career and I have never had any criticism of my computer or literary skills. I am highly competent, efficient, well-mannered, sincere and honest.

To be offered a job and then be pulled up one week later on tests that have no real bearing on whether a person can do a job or not, is in my opinion, a total disgrace and highly unprofessional of you.

You are the owner of a recruitment company. I would have thought that you out of everybody would know what exactly you are looking for and what the job spec is before even interviewing someone, let alone wasting their time on two interviews and then offering them the position.

What you say you wanted is not what you are now saying you want and it is totally unfair and unethical of you to have done this.

I have been searching for a new position for over two months. Based on you offering me a job and then putting it in writing over text telling me how excited you are to be working with me, I rushed the handover period with my boss, which caused an argument and so relations with him have now soured. I wasted one week of my life which could have been put to better use looking for a job where I would actually be appreciated.

You have caused me upset and embarrassment, but more than anything I believe that your behaviour has shown total unprofessionalism which I find appalling and at total odds with your current concerns about how you come across in the business world.

I truly do hope that we both find what we are looking for.

Regards

I now had just over a week to find a job. No pressure then. I couldn't rely on agencies to do this for me. I needed to go straight to the employers directly. I had never used Gumtree for a job before, but as they had recently started to advertise on TV, I thought that perhaps they were now attracting a higher standard of job as opposed to the dodgy, low-paid ones that I imagined existed, prior to TV advertising. I had to at least give it a go.

That evening I scoured the PA and Secretarial section for anything that sounded remotely suitable. I used the same covering email for all, indicating my current salary and what I was looking for in my next role. I didn't want there to be any misunderstanding. A lot of jobs on here didn't tell you what they were offering as a salary, so I needed them to know at the start what I would and would not accept, so as not to waste anyone's time, as I clearly couldn't afford to waste any of my own at this stage. One role in particular stood out for me. It was a property company and they were looking for a PA and Marketing assistant to join them. I had property, PA and advertising experience so it was clearly perfect for me. I applied immediately.

I applied for a handful of other jobs that evening and went to sleep feeling positive. I was on a mission to find something and more determined than ever. The very next day I got an email from a company called Fazakerley, a chartered surveying company. I didn't realise at first, but it was in reply to my application for the PA and marketing assistant job that I had applied for via Gumtree. They wanted to see me for an interview on Monday or Tuesday the next week. I was impressed with their speed. They must have only seen my application that morning and had already arranged dates of when they could do. It didn't seem like this would be a long drawn out process either as they were asking me to meet with three people in the same interview, including the COO.

Thank God. I replied and said I could do the Monday at 9am. The sooner I got to see them, the sooner I would possibly get a job offer. For my own sanity, I needed to know I had a job to go to before I left Arena and I now had one working week to go.

I couldn't afford to keep all my eggs in one basket so I spent that weekend still applying for as many jobs as I could find. I was now avoiding recruitment agencies and instead going for the jugular. Anything was now fair game, even jobs that only required someone for a month or two. I had switched to survival mode and I needed to make money.

I had worked out exactly how long I could possibly live without any work at all, with some savings and Ed's wage. It was probably going to be four months. It wasn't quite panic stations, but it was only a matter of time. Monday's interview was a jewel shining out amongst the debris from the fallout of the last few months. If I paused for breath at any moment, I felt the exhaustion of what I had been through. Was it like this for everyone? Or was I just unusually unlucky? I honestly didn't know how I had survived and got up and kept going every day through the last few months, let alone the last two years. I suppose you just do when you are up against it. Your natural survival instincts kick in and you just keep battling until you reach the end.

So many times in recent months I had made the mistake of thinking I *had* reached the end and just as I had, the carpet had been pulled from underneath my feet. I was so very tired of looking for a job, whilst doing a job and trying to find someone to replace me. I was fed up with the highs and lows and disappointments and false promises from people who should have known better. I needed it to stop. I needed to get this next job and I needed it to be right. I just didn't think I could take much more.

CHAPTER TWENTY SEVEN

I arrived at Fazakerley just before 9am, the following Monday. Their offices were the closer to where I lived than any job I had ever commuted to. A great sign, I thought. The receptionist seemed friendly enough. The décor was suitably modern and I felt at ease. I still hadn't been seen by 9.15am and I was starting to worry as I knew I had to get back to meet the new girl whose arrival I had delayed until 10.30am.

A very tall fat, bald man appeared. He introduced himself as Danny. I couldn't work out his age although I suspected he was in his early forties. He looked like Peter Griffin from *Family Guy*. His face was a friendly, harmless one I thought. Danny was one of the three people who were going to interview me. He apologised that they were running late, but explained that the COO was in another meeting that was over-running. He made a decision to start the interview without him, which I was grateful for. We made our way to a small meeting room where I was introduced to another chap called Martin. He had another friendly, harmless face. We began the interview, which was more like an informal chat. It was brilliant.

They were two of the nicest people I had ever met in an interview. They could not have been more complimentary about my CV and experience, which they thought was 'fantastic'. As they asked me to talk a little about the job I was leaving, Danny had a big grin on his face. I wondered why he was so smiley and then he told me that they knew all about Arena and David Wilkes. They knew exactly what type of a man he was. Apparently David had worked with Fazakerley before and he had completely shafted them, as they described it. The whole company knew of Arena Construction and they all disliked David with a passion. I was so relieved. I didn't need to say anything or make excuses or explain why I wanted to leave after a mere few months. They already knew why. This was going so, so well. Even better than I could have hoped for.

The COO arrived in the room. He apologised if he was about to ask questions that we had already covered, and asked me why I was leaving Arena. Without saying a word, Danny said 'You don't need to ask. We know of David Wilkes and Arena from past dealings with him. The guy is an absolute nightmare'. This job was mine. I felt it. It felt right. Now I just needed to know that they were going to pay a decent enough salary. I was asked if I had any questions. I wanted to know what the hours were and whether I needed a Blackberry out of hours. The hours seemed decent and I wasn't required to carry a Blackberry. Yes! I couldn't bring myself to ask about salary. I'd been taught not to.

Thankfully the COO brought this up as the last point. What were my salary expectations? Hmm. Hadn't they read my covering email? I had clearly set out what I wanted and what I would accept, so to be asked was rather annoying. I said I was on £50,000 and that I had previously been on £40,000, so I was prepared to accept something in between. The COO made a note. He certainly didn't make any noises to indicate that this was way above what they could afford. Our interview came to a close. Danny and Martin were very enthusiastic. We shook hands. I got that familiar feeling again. They wanted me. I wanted them. It was a match.

I was told that they wanted to move quickly and that they were seeing a couple of more people that day, but they would make a decision and let me know the next day at the latest. Wow. This was so good. I truly never expected it to move this quickly, but it is what I needed. Could I really be saved at the last hour? There was now a very strong possibility that I could.

I didn't have to wait until the next day. I was called that afternoon and an offer was made. They loved me and thought I would be a great addition to the team. They were prepared to pay me £42,000. I accepted. I was ecstatic. I had been saved at the last minute.

I almost didn't see David on my last day. He hid in his office until gone 6.30pm and it was only because I was given a small farewell presentation at Arena at the end of the day that I was still there. He saw that a small group of people had gathered. He asked if I had any news on jobs and I was so pleased to be able to tell him that I was off to work for Fazakerley. His face fell on hearing the news. It made me smile inside.

I grabbed David and air kissed him on both cheeks and shook his stiff, craggy hand. He hadn't been expecting that. I am sure I caught him blush. The poor sod just did not know how to deal with normal human beings. He was so far removed from the plebs of society he had no idea how to integrate with us. No wonder he was the way he was. He was probably just completely fucked up inside.

Ah well, it was no longer my problem. I was about to be free of the tyrannous bastard. I walked out of Arena Construction with my head held high and a massive grin on my face. In total I had managed to work there for ten months including my notice period. My future awaited me.

CHAPTER TWENTY EIGHT

My boss is an arsehole. A proper bell-end. I cannot quite believe that it is happening again, but it is. Danny has turned out to be yet another nightmare.

I started at Fazakerley full of beans. On my second day I received the silent treatment from Danny. His mood swings were dreadful. I had to sit opposite him which was frankly, intimidating, because he did nothing but swear at everyone on the team of mostly men, all the time. I discovered in the first week of my new job that the last girl they had employed, had left after six months because she had been bullied by both Danny and Martin, who both turned out to be absolute egomaniacs.

By day four I was in tears in the loos because I felt so overwhelmed by the amount of work they were throwing at me. They had no training in place, yet expected me to know how to use complex specialist design programmes and invoicing systems. Despite me having to talk to the COO about the situation on week two, nothing changed. I had been thrown head first down a toboggan route without a toboggan. I was asked to design stuff on software packages that I had never used. I was asked to attend marketing meetings and events, but felt like a fish out of water. None of this was for me. Not the bosses, the office, nor the workload.

On the first day of my fifth week I was sat in a team meeting, led by Danny, who spent the entire time swearing indirectly at me for things that had gone wrong on a massively important fees spread sheet that I had had no proper training on. I knew he meant it was my fault every time he said 'For fuck's sake'. Everyone else in the room knew he meant me. I was mortified and felt humiliated and belittled. I was on the verge of tears throughout. I was at my absolute lowest ebb.

At the very end of the meeting he turned the attention on me and asked if I was OK with everything. It was done more in an accusatory way than a helpful one though. There was certainly no warmth or mentoring going on in this company. The atmosphere on a daily basis was more like a trading floor. It was hideous. I held back any indication that I was teary. I answered and said that they needed to show me more things and give me proper training. It was true – they needed to tell whoever did this job, how to do it properly. It wasn't going to be me though.

At 5.30pm I grabbed my coat and bag and said goodbye to one of the girls who I had worked with over the last five weeks.

I walked to the nearest bar I could find as my lip trembled and the tears started to well. I ordered the familiar large glass of wine and sat in a private booth where no one could see my tears as they rolled, relentlessly down my face. I called my mum and told her that I couldn't go back. I was about to have a breakdown. I absolutely knew then that I was not going to step foot in Fazakerleys' offices again. Just knowing this made me feel better, but I was far from OK.

That evening, months and months of abuse and pain came to a head and tumbled out of my soul, manifested by tears. I sobbed and sobbed until my eyes were puffy. I drank more and more booze to numb the pain. I didn't want to think of the future as I just couldn't see one. I had no more fight within me. I needed help. I needed to be put to bed and told to rest until better. I couldn't afford to think about bills or money or jobs. I had been treated very badly by three very different people and I was finally broken. It was my mum's call to me later that evening that helped me survive. All I could repeat was that I was a mess. I had made a mess of everything and that *I* was no good at anything. I was weeping.

My poor mum talked me out of my drunken stupor enough to force me to make tea and start thinking clearly. I didn't even have the strength to stop myself from being this way. Normally I would have done anything not to burden my poor mum. It wasn't right that she should still be worrying about her child. I was so very sorry that I was in so much of a mess, but none of it was my fault. I was a kind, sensitive soul who had been trampled on by too many horrible people and

I had simply run out of steam. I was laid out bare in front of her and Ed. I was a wreck; a snivelling, weak, sorry state. Mum made me promise I would call the doctor in the morning, which I did.

I was signed off work for a week and given more sleeping tablets. I told Fazakerley why I had been signed off. They needed to know it was because of the work overload, lack of training and Danny's swearing and general unpleasant attitude. HR didn't seem surprised, but nevertheless could not have been nicer or sorrier that it had happened. Danny kept trying to contact me which stressed me out even further. He finally got the message that *I* would contact *him* when I was ready, after sending him a firm email. I think he was panicked. He wanted *me* to tell *him* that it was OK and that it wasn't his fault that he was a hideous person. I was done making excuses for people though.

Having that week to myself, helped enormously. I slept and ate well. I felt calm and at peace. I didn't know where I was going, but at least I was free. I was too ashamed at first to admit to anyone that I had lasted only five weeks in another job. Towards the end of the week I contacted only agencies who weren't aware I had even left Arena; it was easier not to have to discuss what had just happened and having only been in the job for five weeks, I classed it as a blip and would not even put it on my CV.

I went to a catch up one day, with an agency that had a possible temp to perm job that I thought might be good. I was scared of anything that was permanent. I didn't want to put my name to paper and sign on for another permanent job ever again, unless I knew I wasn't going to be picked on, bullied, treated like dirt or psychologically manipulated. The only way of doing this was by temping and testing the water. I called one more agency after I left my meeting and told them that I fancied temping for a bit as I needed to get some cash. I wasn't expecting anything to happen immediately, but I was transferred to the temp desk straight away. They had something. Something that quite possibly would start the following Tuesday.

I'd heard it all before. Recruitment people were full of it. Always trying to close the deal and keep the carrot dangling. I said I was up for it, whatever it was. They promised to get back to me. I spent my lunch at St Christopher's Place near Bond Street and thought of the crazy, purple-loving, entrepreneur as I walked past his office and laughed to myself. What a lucky escape that had been. There was no snow on this particular day though. The sun had come out and I felt truly relaxed for the first time in months. As I wandered back towards the underground station, my mobile rang. It was the temp desk at the agency. The job was on.

They wanted me to start the following week.

I would be temping, but I also knew that they were looking to fill the role permanently so if I liked it and they liked me, then maybe it would work out? I was so relieved. I went back home and officially resigned from Fazakerley by email.

THE PA'S STORY

From: V Knowles
To: *******, ********
Importance: High
Dear *****

I have now had some time to gather my thoughts and get myself together. I believe that in the long run, the role at Fazakerley is not right for me. To have got to such a state after such a short amount of time really isn't normal as I am sure you will agree.

If I am honest I felt a degree of pressure from the outset when you said that I was expensive and that you would expect me to perform for my salary. It was the only thing that put me off the job at the interview process, but I thought that I would still be able to show you how capable I was and it would work out. However, the amount of work that was given to me in the short space of time I was there, the lack of training and nurturing and the feeling of pressure was simply not something I could cope with ultimately and looking forward, not something that I would like to carry on doing.

Pretty much every single thing that I was asked to do in my time at Fazakerley is not something I had done before and not anything that basic common sense would have got me through. I needed thorough training on how to do invoices, fees, use the agency database etc., none of which was given. On top of that I was also told I was responsible for the group dinners that are on-going plus taking on marketing tasks using software that I absolutely needed training on if I was ever to be up to speed on any of it, all of which simply added more pressure on me.

Had I been given training and had I been nurtured and helped to settle in to the role it may have been a different story, but I unfortunately felt as though I was expected to be up to speed after two weeks.

I feel it would be foolish to stay any longer and waste your time. I thank you very much for the opportunity and I very much enjoyed meeting you and the rest of the Fazakerley team, but please would you accept this email as written confirmation of my notice.

I wish you all the best of luck

Kind regards

The following week I started temping at a company not too far from home. That was where I sat all alone, like a weirdo, in the breakout area, eating my sandwich and dropping crumbs down my coat. That was two years ago.

I am now a permanent member of staff. My boss is the best boss I have ever worked for in my life – he is witty, smart and kind. He encourages me to ask questions and remind him about things because that is what he needs. He doesn't tell me to be quiet or not speak my mind because that would be silencing me and no one should be silenced. We are all important and we should all be allowed to speak freely, wherever we are in life.

In the last year, Rich and Dick have dissolved their own

company, shafting many employees in the process. I still don't think Fashion Designer knows about Rich's philandering ways. I also heard that David Wilkes had the other secretary resign and he sacked Amy's replacement whilst she was signed off sick with stress from his behaviour. I also gather that Fazakerley have never tried to replace me, as I don't think even *they* know what type of person could put up with them.

The company I now work at is one of the kindest, friendliest and most nurturing environments I have ever known. The team of people who I support could not be lovelier. They help each other out, they socialise with each other. We all laugh and talk and make things happen. For the first time in over a decade I feel settled.

I am calm. I sleep well. I wake up and enjoy the journey to work. I no longer have the dreaded Sunday night blues.

This is what it feels like to be happy in your job.

If you don't recognise this feeling, then perhaps it's time you thought about moving on.

Life is too short to spend your time feeling oppressed or scared.

As I know only too well, it is never too late to change.